Be Better Today Than You Were Yesterday!

Tommy Rozycki

Printed in the United States of America

Second Printing, 2017

ISBN 978-1535316866

www.zyckfit.com

Table of Contents

Acknowledgements

I would like to take this opportunity to thank my family, friends, and clients for the constant and undying support through the ups and downs and during all the times I felt unsure of myself. This has been an amazing journey and without you all, I do not know where I would be today. Above all else, I am grateful to God for keeping me on the path to helping and inspiring others.

A special thank you to my client and editor, Tracy Knudsen, for your guidance and help putting this book together. You made this entire process much easier.

A special thank you to my friend and co-worker, Eric Gulizio, for writing the Foreword for this book. Thank you for your constant support and friendship.

A special thank you to my friends and clients for sharing your incredible stories. Each of you embodies what ZyckFit stands for in your own way.

"In everything you do, put God first, and He will direct you and crown your efforts with success."

-Proverbs 3:6

Foreword

by Eric Gulizio

A healthy lifestyle is a lifetime commitment. It requires motivation and action, because a thought alone does not always spark a reaction. What is it that is driving you to make this change? What are your goals? As a personal trainer, I have encountered many different people over the years with a variety of goals. One thing that every one of them had in common is that they all decided to make a commitment.

Fitness has come a long way over the years. It has evolved from a fad without much scientific research to back it, into an absolute necessity. Before you can begin your journey towards a healthy lifestyle, you must possess a need, a desire, to be successful. It all starts with a goal. This goal must be clear and attainable. That is the reason why the most important parts of the process are action and motivation.

Let's start with a simple definition of the word motivation. "Motivation is the reason or reasons one has for acting or behaving in a particular way." Why are you driven? Being a personal trainer for over fifteen years, I have been a part of some wonderful, and some not so wonderful, journeys. Some of these individuals were in dire need of losing large amounts of weight to literally save his or her life. Others, for simply vanity, wanted to be a flawless, aesthetic picture of perfection. Of course, there have also been many who were concerned with the future of their health and wanted to implement preventative measures. Were all of these stories, stories of success? Unfortunately, no they were not. To succeed, we must be accountable for both our thoughts and our actions.

Once you have chosen your goal(s), you need to ensure that you will stay motivated. You cannot remain motivated without taking responsibility. Accountability is the obligation we owe ourselves to act on our goals. If you are not in the right frame of mind to be successful, and to turn thoughts into actions, then you will not succeed.

The future is unpredictable. We cannot predict our own success, or anyone else's for that matter. There are tools, however, that you can utilize to greatly improve your chances of success. One of my favorites, and, to me, the most important, is not allowing the fear of failure to stop you. Some of the most successful people throughout history have had to experience failure in order to achieve greatness. If you are able to transfer your fear of failure into a positive thought, it can become a powerful tool in building your future.

Taking steps day-by-day, and keeping them in perspective, is important for long-term results. Achieving small accomplishments along the way will help you stay motivated towards reaching overall success. Discipline in your daily life is necessary in order to stay committed to your goals. Make it a habit to ask yourself, "What have I done today that contributed to my overall goal?" and you will become closer to success each passing day!

The ZyckFit lifestyle and mentality will help both the seasoned athlete as well as the average person develop a plan of attack to determine and achieve goals throughout all areas of life. Tommy Rozycki has developed more than a brand. ZyckFit is a concept that expands beyond merely fitness and getting in shape. ZyckFit encompasses many vital components required to live a rewarding and fulfilling life. In addition to being a seasoned personal trainer, Tommy is a first-class motivator and a driven entrepreneur. He has put his heart and soul into "Be Better Today Than You Were Yesterday!" which is surely the debut of more exciting and motivational work to follow in the years ahead. If you are stuck in a rut or just need to take some areas of your life to the next level, ZyckFit and "Be Better Today Than You Were Yesterday!" will undoubtedly provide the tools and the mental boost you need to reach your full potential!

Preface

The intention of this book is to guide, inspire, and motivate people from all walks of life to improve the quality of their lives through fitness and overall wellness. After reading this book, I hope you acquire a new outlook on, not only changing your own life, but on changing the lives of others as well!

ZyckFit was created with the purpose of helping individuals of all ages and fitness levels reach their full potential both physically and mentally. Too often, we do not realize how much we are capable of accomplishing during our lifetime. In many instances, self-doubt or fear of failure cripples an individual's ambition to pursue their dreams or goals. Sometimes, an outside source or stimulus is required to awaken this potential. This stimulus may be an event, a conversation, or even a movie. I hope this book will be that source of inspiration for you.

Personally, I knew writing a book would be pointless if I did not have an audience to read it. At the time, I was brand new in the fitness industry and had not written anything since college just a few years earlier. I needed an identity and a brand people could recognize and get behind, a brand that stood for something inspirational and genuine. I decided I would create a logo and start a weekly blog, to not only grow my audience, but to also hone my writing skills. I chose the name ZyckFit, derived from Rozycki, because I have tremendous respect for my family name and I believe it is important to always remember where you came from. To me, the name Rozycki stands for compassion, work ethic, and reliability. Therefore, ZyckFit stands for just that: compassion, work ethic, and reliability.

Rather quickly, ZyckFit evolved into much more than just a blog. I received support from friends, family, clients, and individuals in my community who knew how much potential ZyckFit possessed. And I believe ZyckFit has the potential to impact people not only locally, but globally as well! Growing ZyckFit to where it is today has become an arduous journey I did not see coming, and it has forced me to learn a great deal about business, life, and myself in general. I never knew how much I was capable of until I started chasing this dream. I encourage you, the reader, to do the same regardless of how big or out of reach your dream may seem. Only then, will you find out who you truly are.

Currently, ZyckFit LLC. is helping individuals improve their lives through personal training, online training, fitness boot camps, community events, and public speaking engagements. With the help of this book, ZyckFit will make an ongoing positive impact on the lives of individuals of all ages around the world.

Looking to the future, I hope to see ZyckFit influencing individuals in their daily lives. I envision people around the world wearing ZyckFit apparel, hash tagging ZyckFit on their social media posts, and making changes to their lives thanks to ZyckFit. If ZyckFit can teach others to live more compassionate, fulfilling and selfless lives, then I have accomplished my mission.

So, if you know you want more out of life and are not quite sure how to get started, let today serve as a new beginning for yourself. Also, if this is your first time reading this book, please keep in mind that the ideas and lessons discussed throughout these chapters require time, practice, and discipline. Trust the process and never settle for anything less than you think you deserve. It's now time to start living the life you were meant to live.

Never stop Learning, Never stop Growing, Never stop Improving!

Part I: Where to Begin…

Chapter 1: What is ZyckFit?

"There is nothing noble in being superior to your fellow man; true nobility is being superior to your former self."

\- Ernest Hemingway

Every day we are faced with a number of choices. These choices affect our current situation, our future, and even the lives of those around us in either a positive or a negative way. Being ZyckFit allows you to recognize these choices, and their consequences, and to act accordingly.

So what exactly is ZyckFit, pronounced Zick-Fit, you may be wondering? If you have been following my journey until now, then you should already have a pretty good idea. For those of you who have never heard of ZyckFit, you will soon learn through reading this book that ZyckFit is a way of life encompassing a balance of physical, mental, and spiritual health.

First and foremost, ZyckFit is a personal training company focused on improving the overall well-being of others. Fitness and Wellness is a popular and consistently evolving trend in society. People are becoming better educated and more aware of how and why they should take care of their health. Advances in technology, including apps and gadgets, are helping individuals become healthier in their everyday lives. To be ZyckFit includes understanding the importance of taking care of your body through proper nutrition, exercise, and rest. To a further extent, being ZyckFit requires making sacrifices in return for the betterment of the body including: making consistent workouts a priority, getting enough sleep for rest and recovery, and making a conscious effort to eat a balanced diet. Only through discipline and wise decision-making can we hope to overcome the tough choices we are faced with on a daily basis. For most people, sticking to a strict workout schedule, choosing sleep over going out or staying up late, and eating healthy instead of eating junk food can be difficult. I completely understand why these choices are difficult to make, as I have faced them myself, but they are necessary in order to see results.

Every year, millions of people die due to complications related to Obesity, Diabetes, and High Blood Pressure. Risk factors associated with these diseases can be alleviated and even eliminated through exercise and a healthy diet. Benefits of a healthy lifestyle include not only looking and feeling good, but also being healthy physically, as well as mentally. Does it take hard work to see results? Yes. Does it take a lot of sacrifice to see a difference? Yes. Is your health and quality of life worth it? Definitely!

The body cannot rely on physical health alone, mental health is equally essential for total wellness. To be ZyckFit includes waking up every day with a positive mindset, a mindset ready to take on the new challenges and adventures of the day. To get motivated, start each day off with an empowering mantra to prepare yourself for what you want to accomplish that day. The alarm clock message on my phone every morning reads "Rise and Grind! Be better today than you were yesterday!" One of the most important lessons I have learned in life so far is to find the positive side of every situation. If you look hard enough, no matter how difficult it may seem, you can take a positive lesson away from anything life throws at you. Remember, with a ZyckFit mentality, you never lose, you either win or you learn!

In addition to staying positive, it is important to keep the mind active. For children and teenagers, keeping the mind active will stimulate and improve the synapses within the brain. For adults and seniors, keeping the mind active will keep the mind sharp to help ward off memory loss and dementia. Some ideas to keep your mind active are reading, playing an instrument, listening to music, or downloading apps on your phone that are mentally stimulating. Also, do not be afraid to "unplug" from technology from time to time. Go for a walk or start a new hobby. An active mind is a healthy mind. And, a thriving, healthy mind will promote clear thinking, productivity, and a positive mood.

As someone with a background in Psychology and experience working with the mentally ill, I can confidently say that many of us take our own Mental Health for granted. It is a goal of mine to eventually start a 5K race or some other type of event to help raise money and awareness to help those suffering from mental illness.

Furthermore, the mind and body are nothing without a connection to the spirit. To be ZyckFit includes being in tune with your inner self, your life force, your soul, whatever you want to call it. Regardless of your beliefs, you cannot deny the fact that there is something deeper than flesh, which can push an individual to accomplish amazing feats. A person's spirit can withstand oppression or persecution, help surpass physical limitations, and even evoke inspiration within others. To create and deepen this bond requires meditation and self-reflection. At least once a day, make sure to take a minimum of 10-15 minutes to do nothing but breathe and collect your thoughts. Envision what you want in life and the steps it will take to acquire it. The point of these short periods of "me time" is to help you focus your mind and to also relieve stress. For those who do believe in a higher power or a deity, this is a great time to pray or to count your blessings. As you strengthen the connection between your mind, body, and spirit, you will become more powerful and unstoppable than you previously thought possible.

For as long as I can remember, I have always had two unwavering dreams: to write a book and to educate others. Upon entering college at the University of Central Florida, I originally intended to study to become an elementary school teacher. But after only one semester, I switched my focus to Psychology with the dream of becoming a Marriage and Family Therapist. After graduating with my Bachelor's Degree in Psychology and working in a mental health clinic for two years, I realized I wanted to change my career focus yet again to another one of my passions, Fitness! Sports and physical activity have always been a huge part of my life. I spent most of my time during my earlier years playing outside and I have always excelled at a variety of sports. It helps that I am an extremely competitive individual and am always up for a challenge! In 2014, I moved back to my hometown of Jupiter, Florida where I researched various personal training certifications. After comparing several of the more popular and well-known learning institutions, I decided that NASM, the National Academy of Sports Medicine, was the right certification for me. Currently, I am employed at ZBody Strength & Fitness, a local Personal Training studio where I am free to run and grow my business as I see fit. Personal Training has allowed me to transform individuals, not only physically, but mentally as well. I do my best to connect personally with each one of my clients so we may break down barriers as we work together to accomplish their individual goals!

Have you noticed an underlying theme yet? I love helping people. Whether that person is a family member, a friend, a client, or even a stranger, nothing makes me feel better than knowing I have helped another person in a positive way. In fact, I always say that true success comes, not from how much money you make, but by how many people you help. ZyckFit is all about being the best you can be. Period. If you improve yourself every day, whether it is physically, mentally, spiritually, socially, or financially, you will find true happiness one day, it is inevitable! You cannot be afraid to ask yourself what it is you truly want out of life and then go after it. Life is too short and there are too many opportunities in the world for you to not chase your dreams!

That being said, I originally created ZyckFit in September 2014 in hopes of building an audience for this book and for any other endeavors God may put in my path, all while helping others along the way. I told myself that as long as I truly impacted at least one person's life through ZyckFit, all the hard work would be worth it. I believe I was put on earth to help people; it is what makes me truly happy. Since ZyckFit's inception, I have created and run fitness boot camps for both children and adults, been featured in news publications, written a weekly blog, trained clients online nationwide, and have participated in local events throughout my community, along with a number of other ventures. The most satisfying aspect of these accomplishments has been the ability to give back to the community that raised me and has given me so much.

I am a huge believer in giving back to the community. In a day and age where everyone is breaking their neck to get ahead, we tend to forget to give back to our community and to those who helped or supported us throughout the years. The area we grew up in and the area we live when we're older supply us with employment, good times, loved ones, and opportunities to grow. The least we can do is give back a little bit of our time and energy. Try to make time to volunteer at your center of worship, mentor an underprivileged child, or donate clothes to a homeless shelter. "In everything I did, I showed you that by this kind of hard work we must help the weak, remembering the words the Lord Jesus himself said: 'It is more blessed to give than to receive.'"- Acts 20:35

Throughout this book, you will find powerful quotes, a collection of my experiences that I hope you will be able to relate to personally, and stories from individuals who have been impacted by ZyckFit. I hope you will take at least one lesson from these chapters and use it to make a positive impact on your daily life. That is what ZyckFit is all about, taking steps every day, both large and small, in order to better yourself and those around you.

Chapter 2: Let's Get Started!

"Do not go where the path may lead, go instead where there is no path and leave a trail."

- Ralph Waldo Emerson

Making a change, even when we know it will benefit us, is seldom easy. Humans are creatures of habit, and altering our usual routine can be difficult. Stepping out of our comfort zone is never simple. Many of us possess a fear of failure, so we tend to stick with what we are used to rather than to face the unknown. Whether we are apprehensive about joining a gym, worried about changing career paths, or afraid of the idea of failing if we try something new, the truth of the matter is we must all begin somewhere. Taking the first step towards making a change tends to be the hardest part of the journey for many individuals.

My fitness journey started in Beginner's Weightlifting class at Jupiter High School when I was sixteen-years-old. I had never lifted weights before and I certainly did not have the best eating habits. Most guys my age were already bigger and stronger than I was, but I did not let that discourage me. Results would not come overnight and I understood this. I immediately took a liking to weightlifting and I began looking forward to that class each day more than any other. I grew up playing sports, so my body adapted to lifting weights fairly quickly. At the time, I was playing basketball after school just about every day and lifting weights helped improve my strength, speed, and jumping ability. As time went by, I began to notice I was getting bigger, leaner, and stronger. That is when I fell in love with working out. There are few things in life more rewarding than seeing the progress your body makes as a result of the hard work you put it through. To me, there is no feeling in the world that compares to how you feel after you complete a tough workout or win a competition. As soon as I started seeing results, I was hooked!

After a couple years of learning the fundamentals of weight lifting in high school, I took what I learned with me to the University of Central Florida in Orlando, Florida. Throughout college, I increased my training intensity and began working out 6-7 days a week. In addition to lifting weights more frequently, I began playing Intramural Sports and taking Group Fitness classes at the school's facilities, my favorite being Yoga. Group Fitness classes improved my balance, coordination, stamina, and core strength -- benefits I was not receiving solely from resistance training. In addition to being a great workout, Yoga helped me focus my mind and work on breathing techniques, both of which I find incredibly helpful outside of the gym as well. My college workout partners, consisting of roommates and friends, taught me a great deal over the next four years, increasing my knowledge and helping add variety to my diet and workouts.

After graduating from UCF, I had no choice but to switch to a local gym where I would go without a workout partner for the next three years. During this time, my jobs and my social life had a negative impact on my workouts. I was working long hours between multiple jobs and partying too much on the weekends. I was going to the gym just to go to the gym and I wasn't seeing much progress. Eventually, I made the decision to move back home to Jupiter, Florida, which turned out to be just the change I needed! As I said goodbye to working in the mental health field, I combined what I had learned about Psychology and fitness over the years with what I would soon learn during my personal training certification process to form my personal training style.

Transitioning into a career as a personal trainer was surprisingly smooth for me, as this career has allowed me to combine my three passions: education, therapy, and fitness. My background in Psychology and my love for teaching have assisted me in understanding what my clients are going through and granted me the patience to help them transform both physically and mentally. It is quite rewarding to see a client carry him or herself with more confidence as the pounds drop off or to receive texts full of excitement after a client is told good news about their health from their doctor. Personal training is not just about making people look good; it is a powerful tool of motivation and guidance that changes people's lives in a number of ways. Personal training allows me to help individuals live happier, healthier lives, and that is what I have always wanted in a career.

Living a healthy lifestyle requires both patience and discipline. A healthy lifestyle is more than just a short-term diet to lose a few stubborn pounds or a few months of working out to get ready for a special occasion. A healthy lifestyle is a lifelong commitment consisting of day-to-day choices that will benefit your well-being for as long as you live.

To help yourself along your journey of healthy living, it is imperative that you set realistic goals targeted specifically for you. It helps to write your goals down so you can physically see and reflect on them every day. This will make you feel more inclined to work towards these goals wholeheartedly. You know the saying "out of sight, out of mind", so if you are not regularly reviewing and adjusting your goals, they will eventually fall apart. I prefer to keep my list of goals on my phone so it can be accessed and edited at any time.

Some people want to quit smoking, some want to lose weight, and others may want to get a new job, go back to school, or try out for a sports team. Whatever your goal(s) may be, even if you share a similar goal with someone you know, your mentality or way of accomplishing that goal may not be the same as him or her. At the end of the day, you must be able to rely on yourself to keep going, even when the odds seem to be stacked against you. People *will* disappoint you throughout your life. Therefore you must believe in *yourself* and *your* potential. Realistic goals are the framework for success; to be without them is like wandering through the woods with no compass, you have no direction.

Life is all about resilience and how you react to different situations. Well-known and respected Christian pastor, author, and educator, Charles R. Swindoll, said, "Life is ten percent what happens to you and ninety percent how you respond to it." Life is far from perfect. You are not going to reach every goal you

14

ever set by its deadline, but that does not mean you should be disappointed with yourself or give up on accomplishing it. If anything, not meeting a goal should motivate you to work even harder. Successful people learn from their failures. A failure is a negative experience only if you allow it to be. What can you do differently? What can you take from this setback to succeed next time? Reflect on your progress, appreciate how far you have come, re-assess what changes you must make or how long it will take to reach your goal, and then continue working hard until you achieve it!

You must always keep in mind that a healthy lifestyle is a marathon and not a sprint. You will not see results overnight. You did not get to where you are right now in a week or two, so you should not expect to see progress right away either. There is no magic pill for success. Trust the process and put in the hard work; you will feel a much greater sense of pride knowing you accomplished your goals the right way.

Once you have your goals wisely mapped out, you can now start working towards them. Depending on your personality and what you are trying to accomplish, you will have to decide which route will be the most effective and most logical one for you to take. For some, success may depend on meeting the right contacts, whereas for others it may mean dedicating every single day to practicing to become the best at their sport. Success never comes the same way for two different people. We each have our own paths to the top, filled with detours, dead ends, and sometimes shortcuts. Along our journey, we must keep our eyes on the finish line, make connections with individuals who can help us, and be strong enough to eliminate the things that hold us back.

Again, there is more to being ZyckFit than just a healthy lifestyle. To be ZyckFit means to be the best you can be in all areas of your life. Do you surround yourself with people who want you to be successful? Are you where you want to be in life financially? Do you use your time to the best of your ability every day? Regardless of your current status in life, there is always plenty of room for improvement.

Contrary to popular belief, progress usually does not require extreme overnight action. Changes that last a lifetime often require small, careful steps that build a strong foundation and help avoid relapse. For myself, I know if I try to break a habit cold turkey or attempt to dive right into something too quickly, the momentum is almost always impossible to maintain. Once I realize my mistake, I make the necessary adjustments so I will be able to sustain the new lifestyle change. For example, in the past, every time I tried to make a drastic change to my eating habits, I tended to go overboard and ended up reverting back to my old ways. Whenever this happens, I gradually replace one unhealthy eating habit with a healthier option, making the change virtually unnoticeable to my daily routine. Although I no longer miss the old, unhealthy eating habit, the change I made is passively having a positive effect on my well-being over time.

The same thought process applies to money, if you do a complete 180° with the way you are used to living and spending, you are going to most likely either begin hating life or eventually give in and indulge with a shopping spree. Instead, if you start taking a portion of your paycheck and put it aside, you will gradually accumulate a nice savings without feeling the loss in your pockets. Financial discipline has become easier today with online banking and direct deposit, because now you can automatically allocate a desired amount of your paycheck into your savings instead of having to battle your impulses every time you get paid. Create a budget to separate your necessities from your luxuries. Only then will you be able to cut out unnecessary expenses. Make it easier on yourself by developing a system to secure a better future for you and your loved ones.

Communication is an important element of being human and a key element of the ZyckFit lifestyle. Not one of us communicates exactly the same as someone else. The world contains introverts, extraverts, and those who fall somewhere in between. Communicating and networking come easier for some than for others. And, in today's growing world of technology, you don't even need to interact with people face-to-face anymore. Personally, I consider myself primarily an extravert with introverted tendencies. I like to think of myself as a people person, yet I still enjoy doing many activities on my own. My personality and communication skills have always helped me when meeting new people, assisting customers, and building personal and professional relationships.

Every single person you meet in life has at least one lesson to offer if you are receptive enough to learn from him or her. Even before starting my own company, I always looked for new opportunities to connect with people to learn more, experience more, and network with even more people through them. I have met many of my closest friends through a mutual friend. Social media and the Internet have made it easier than ever to meet and stay in touch with friends new and old. A new job or romantic relationship could be just one connection away. So get out there and start communicating!

Again, I'm not saying to overwhelm yourself and try to befriend every person you come into contact with. Instead, take meeting new people one step at a time. Throughout your day, look for opportunities to make new acquaintances. Spark up a conversation with the Starbucks barista you see every morning or try linking up with a classmate to become study buddies. If you make small gestures to get to know the people who are already around you on a daily basis, then you will have an easy way to initiate a conversation with them. Who knows, maybe those people have been too shy to start a conversation with *you* all this time! Every time you begin a new relationship, you create the possibility to add a link to your professional network or to start a lifelong friendship. If you are shy and social media is more your style, try looking through your mutual friends on Facebook or searching for people on other platforms with similar interests as you to create digital friendships. The world is at your fingertips; your new best friend could be looking for you from another continent! One way or another, step out of your comfort zone and starting meeting new people today.

Physicist and author, Stephen Hawking said, "Intelligence is the ability to adapt to change." Sadly, I feel most people do not value intelligence as highly as they do other things. I have always enjoyed learning and I believe the more you know, the more opportunities will become available to you. As cliché as it sounds, I truly believe knowledge is power. When you are well versed in a variety of subjects, you become more appealing during job interviews, you are able to carry on more meaningful conversations with others, and you are better prepared to solve problems when you are faced with challenges. When we limit our hunger for knowledge, we are robbing ourselves of potential answers and possibilities. Never allow yourself to become stagnant or apathetic in your search for knowledge.

For many, the quest for knowledge ends after high school or college. Others, though, believe that with age comes wisdom and we naturally improve and learn more as we get older. However, knowledge is simply not acquired through aging, but through experience and actively searching for it. The creation of the Internet has revolutionized the way we learn, study, and acquire information. Encyclopedias have become obsolete and we now carry (and wear) devices with Internet capability on us at all times. Today, anyone with access to a computer is capable of learning about any topic they so choose for free. Children are learning advanced topics at a younger age and more adults are returning to school than ever before. The information is available; you just have to be willing to look for it. What else can you do to improve your intellect? Read books, pick up a new hobby, start playing a musical instrument, or learn a new language. Challenge yourself to expand your horizons. The world is a big place with a lot of history and it is changing rapidly. There are an endless number of topics for you to start learning about; get started today!

I consider myself to be a spiritual person. In my case, I mean that primarily in a religious way. That being said, I do not believe you have to have any particular set of beliefs to connect with your inner spirit. To me, the true power of the human spirit is indefinable by science or inconceivable to the human mind. The spirit is the thing deep inside each of us that can be our greatest weapon or our biggest weakness in life. At times, the mind and body waver, yet the spirit endures. When all hope seems lost, on days when we feel like giving up, the spirit urges us to hold on just a little bit longer.

Personal beliefs aside, I rely on my spirit all the time, whether I am struggling with personal issues, needing an extra push to get through a workout, or looking for fortitude when faced with adversity. To strengthen and preserve my spirit, I try to pray and meditate as often as I feel the need to. At times, this may only be for a few minutes during a short break in a long day full of clients. I like to use Yoga as an opportunity to regroup and refocus while also strengthening my mind and body. My parents taught me to pray before bed every night when I was a child and I still do to this day. Not only is this a perfect time to give thanks to God, it also helps me to reflect on my day and to end my night peacefully. Our mind and spirit are often barraged with negativity through failures, mistakes, and daily frustrations both in and out of our control. For this reason, it is important to take time to counteract these deterrents with breathing techniques, tranquility, and positive thinking.

Starting a new task or venture doesn't have to be as intimidating as it may seem. If you take the proper steps and move at the appropriate pace, you can achieve anything you set your mind to. The important thing is to *take* that first step. Like the legendary Wayne Gretzky said, "You miss 100% of the shots you don't take." This is your life story, make it one worth telling!

I Am ZyckFit: Angie's Story

Growing up, I had the metabolism every girl envied. I was able to eat anything I wanted and never gain a pound. Maybe it was my genetics, youth, activity level as a gymnast and cheerleader, or a combination of all three.

After the birth of my daughter, at age 23, I was fortunate enough to lose all but 10 pounds of the pregnancy weight I had gained. A short time later, though, I began to gain weight. The more weight I gained, the more depressed I became. And the more depressed I became, the more weight I gained. The most ironic part of the situation was that I opened up a personal training studio with my husband. He ran the business while I continued to work as a teacher. I was too embarrassed to work out at our own gym; always thinking my husband would be ashamed that I, "the fat wife", was representing our business. So, I stayed away from the gym and cried every time I stepped on the scale. I hit an all-time low when my husband left me and I found myself as a single mother at 33 years old. I never wanted to step inside a gym again, or on a scale for that matter. I did not want to be reminded of all the beautiful, thin, sexy women my husband would train at our business.

However, in the midst of my depression, I had no appetite, which resulted in me losing a significant amount of weight. I felt terrible on the inside but looked great on the outside. Years later, I met my present husband and found happiness again. But, with happiness, came the weight once again. Finally, one Christmas, I asked my husband for the gift that I wanted more than anything: a personal trainer. I promised my husband and myself that I would change my life if I could just meet a person who could motivate me to be the person I used to be. That person was Tommy Rozycki of ZyckFit!

Being in a gym again brought back such bad memories: the smell of sweat, the sound of weights slamming, and thin women who I thought obviously didn't need to go to the gym. All of this did a number on my psyche. But, I was determined to leave the past in the past and start a new life. I trained with Tommy three times a week. We made daily, weekly, and monthly goals together. He kept track of measurements and we celebrated as the inches dropped and the muscles grew. His constant encouragement made me feel like I could do anything! His mantra, "Be Better Today Than You Were Yesterday" became a constant reminder in my head anytime I thought of quitting.

When a fitness competition took place at the gym, I jumped at the chance to participate. Although I did not win the competition, I could not believe the gains I had made: body fat percentage and inches decreased and my lean muscle mass increased. Tommy was able to explain to me once and for all, that the number on the scale did *not* represent my fitness level. I finally understood that a number did not determine all of my accomplishments. Tommy encouraged me for an entire year to trust him, to push harder, and to never stop improving. By taking what I learned from Tommy and ZyckFit, my life changed in so many other ways!

Not only was Tommy a fantastic trainer, but also he is Catholic, like me. We shared stories of our faith, and this common thread we shared uplifted me even more. To add even more of a benefit to my life, Tommy also has experience in the mental health field, and is very knowledgeable about Depression. Tommy understood me physically, mentally, and spiritually. How could I have been so blessed? I truly believe God sent me Tommy: a person I so desperately needed in my life to uplift me and restore my confidence once again.

How has ZyckFit impacted my life? In more ways than I can count and deserve!

Chapter 3: Living Healthy With a Busy Schedule

"Success usually comes to those who are too busy to be looking for it."

- Henry David Thoreau

For as long as I can remember, I have always enjoyed the feeling of being busy. I have always been a goal-oriented, focused individual. Even on my rest days from the gym and work, I enjoy being productive. Don't get me wrong, I appreciate relaxing as well, but getting things done is much more satisfying in the long run. There is always something you can be doing to improve the current situation you are in; you just have to be willing to put in the time and effort. Life is short and the world doesn't owe you anything, so if you want something, it is up to you to earn it!

Like many of you, I find myself constantly wishing there were more hours in the day in order to get everything I need done. Between sleeping, running errands, completing chores, and working, finding time to do things for ourselves can be tough. Despite the struggle, we must do our best to create a balance in order to ensure that everyone and everything we hold dear is taken care of.

Finding Time

The most common excuse you will hear when you ask people why they do not exercise regularly is lack of time. We're human, I get it, and there are only so many hours in a day. In an ideal world, we would all be superheroes where we could balance our work, school, family time, social life, *and* still have plenty of energy to get in a quality workout. As you know, the real world is unpredictable, and quite often, we do not have control over what is going on around us. That being said, we can still make the best of what time we *do* have under our control.

Making time to exercise must be a priority. If it isn't already one for you, make it one. There are a number of benefits, both mental and physical, attributed to exercising. Not only is it important for staying healthy, it can help you relieve the stress from your day. If you are a morning person, get your workout in early and start your day off in a positive way. You will feel energized and get your metabolism fired up for the day. If it helps, block your schedule for the gym or an outdoor activity as you would for a nail appointment or a doctor's visit. When you don't set aside time to work out, it becomes much easier to skip. When you skip the gym once, it becomes much easier to make it a habit. Even if you only exercise for 30 minutes that is 30 minutes better spent than sitting on the couch. Remember: "The only bad workout is the one that didn't happen."

An effective method for discovering free time is to create a "Time Journal." A Time Journal will assist you in breaking down your schedule in order to weed out any free time that could be used more productively. Monitor how you use your time over a week or two and decide how you can use it more efficiently. You may not even be aware of how much time you spend watching TV or sleeping in until you see it written out in front of you. Once you have an idea of how much free time you have at your disposal, you can begin assigning time to read, exercise, help your children with their homework, or any other activity you choose; just make sure it is constructive.

Even busy parents can find ways to incorporate being active while spending time with their children. Walking, playing, and riding bikes after school and work are a few great ways to enjoy time together and still complete the minimum recommended 30 minutes of daily activity. So not only are you reaping the benefits, but so are your children! It is important to instill values such as living a healthy lifestyle on your children as early on as possible. This way, they will not have to learn these habits later on in adulthood. It is our responsibility as adults to raise educated, conscientious individuals who will strive to make the world a better place.

A Healthy Workplace

Unfortunately, responsibilities and indulgences require us to work for a living thus taking up a fair share of our daily lives. People spend a great portion of their adult years working one or more jobs in order to afford a living for their loved ones. Although a job is essential to provide both necessities and luxuries, the workplace can be a source of stress, frustration, and sadness for many individuals. Because you are spending a large amount of time at work, it is imperative for your mental and physical health to find ways to make your time spent there more enjoyable. If your occupation does not leave you fulfilled, it is time to look for another job immediately. You cannot afford to get stuck in a dead-end job for the next few decades. Yes, money is important, but your health and happiness are invaluable. Yes, your job pays the bills that keep food on the table and a roof over your family's heads, but you will end up putting your loved ones at risk if your health diminishes and they are faced with exorbitant hospital or funeral bills.

Millions of people around the world work in offices and spend the majority of their day sitting at a desk or in front of a computer. One of the biggest health risks that comes from working in an office setting is sitting for hours at a time. Sitting for extended periods not only ensures that you are not being active and moving around, it also gradually affects your spine and your gut. When we are constantly sitting, the discs in our back become compressed; this can eventually become a problem for your posture, flexibility, and mobility. In addition, being sedentary day in and day out at work will eventually add up on your waistline. When possible, try to take short walks or stretch breaks throughout the day. Try occasionally replacing your office chair with a stability ball in order to challenge your core muscles and to practice sitting up straight instead of slouching forward. Also, keep a water bottle in sight on your desk to make sure you stay hydrated throughout the day.

The workplace, especially in an office setting, can be a very social environment. Co-workers frequently bring in snacks before or during work and sometimes go out to happy hour for drinks afterwards to unwind and build friendships among their peers. I fully support a social atmosphere at work and know firsthand how important it is to blow off steam and build rapport with your co-workers. But, try to limit happy hour to once a week to avoid excess calories due to alcoholic beverages and restaurant meals. As far as snacks in the break room, suggest fruit baskets or veggie platters to your peers instead of donuts and cookies. You may be surprised how much the little things add up when trying to live a healthier lifestyle.

As I mentioned before, the workplace can be a source of frustration and stress for many people. In time, this can add up and result in becoming burned out. "Burnout" is usually characterized by fatigue, lack of motivation or enthusiasm, and decreased productivity. I know because this is how I began to feel after working in a mental health clinic for two years. Naturally, I am a hard-worker with remarkable people skills. I typically enjoy going to work, interacting with customers, mingling with co-workers, and doing my best to help the company succeed. However, when I would work for months straight without a day off or allow my job consume me to the point that I was bringing the emotional baggage home with me, I began to notice I was dozing off at my desk, keeping my conversations with clients brief, and sometimes even dreading going to work the next day. I knew I needed a change, so I weighed my options of applying to grad school, finding a new job, or taking a leap of faith by moving back home and starting in a new field. The last option turned out to be one of the best decisions I have ever made.

If you find yourself feeling burned out at work or are heading in that direction, here is what I suggest doing before looking for a new job. Begin each day with a positive attitude, greet co-workers and clients with a smile, and don't let the small stuff get to you. If you allow it, a small incident or one rude customer can snowball and ruin your entire day or week. Be sure to take small breaks throughout the day to meditate, clear your mind, and to simply breathe. Remember, your job is not your life; it is there to pay your bills and to provide financial freedom. A bad day at work is not the end of the world. Keep in mind that your current position should be merely a stepping stone or a temporary gig until you finish school, a promotion opens up, or until you figure out what you want to do for the rest of your life. Give every day your all and people will notice. A solid work ethic and outstanding customer service will get you far.

A Healthy Homelife

The saying "Home is where the heart is" has always rang true to me. In my opinion, there is no greater gift in the world than our family. Our family consists of the people who shape who we are from the time we are born. Our first memories and lessons come from time spent with our family members. No matter our age, we each have a role in contributing to our family's well-being. Adults play the part of protectors, teachers, and caregivers for children. Parents are responsible for teaching their kids how to become responsible members of society, as well as how to live a long, fulfilling life. Among these lessons should include proper eating habits, the benefits of exercising, and the importance of perpetually seeking knowledge. Although children begin their lives in a student role, they often take on the role of guardian and caregiver as our parents get older. Even at a young age, children can help out in one way or another. Kids can relieve some of the workload around the house by completing a variety of chores. With the proper system in place, this can be a great way to teach your children lessons pertaining to work ethic and responsibility. In some families, the children may be more educated and aware of the importance of fitness and nutrition, making it their responsibility to pass this knowledge on to the older generations.

Whether one person or the entire family is trying to lose weight or get into shape, it will take a group effort to help reach the desired goals. One weak link can sabotage the entire household. Temptations in the form of junk food, alcohol, and sugary drinks should be removed immediately. You are much stronger as a unit and must be there for one another in times of need. Go for walks together, take the family grocery shopping, look for local, recreational, family-oriented activities online-- whatever it takes to keep everyone cohesive and motivated!

Although exercise is important for a healthy lifestyle, nutrition is a major part of the battle as well. Meal prep is not only a time saver; it can help prevent unhealthy decisions throughout the week. Cooking meals yourself is the best way to ensure that you and your family are receiving quality food without all of the additives you get when you order take-out or eat at restaurants. Unfortunately, the cooking process can take more time than desired which is not ideal after a long day or when you have to wake up early the next day. Prepping meals with your children is a great way to teach them healthy eating habits and the impact of nutrition, or lack thereof, on the body. Develop a system together that will make meals easy and efficient throughout the week. An alternative to meal prep is pre-made food delivery services. Although this may be a more expensive option, you are guaranteed a healthy variety of foods that are ready to be heated up or taken on the go.

Staying Healthy While Travelling

Every now and then, I have clients who travel quite often and they ask me what they can do to stay healthy while on the road. My first suggestion is to always pack vitamins. You are constantly bombarded by germs while traveling, so it is imperative to keep your immune system strong, especially if you are traveling internationally. Keep hand sanitizer on you and make sure to wash your hands with soap and water whenever possible. Make sure to stay adequately hydrated as well by drinking plenty of water, especially when flying. Regarding exercise, hotels and cruise ships usually have some type of fitness center so you do not have to miss any workouts. Although you will most likely have a lot to do, try to get a sufficient amount of sleep each night. If you are on a road trip, pull over every so often to stretch and walk around. Take advantage of new locations and scenery to try activities you aren't normally able to do at home. Get creative and have some fun being active while travelling abroad!

Getting Adequate Rest

A good night of sleep is essential for the body and mind to feel refreshed and rejuvenated and to prepare us for the day ahead. It is true not everyone requires the same amount of sleep to function properly, but the recommended amount is anywhere from 6-8 hours each night for adults and 9-11 hours for children. A satisfactory amount of sleep puts us in a better mood and allows the mind to stay sharp throughout the day. Proper sleep also aids in weight control, boosts the immune system, and allows muscles to rebuild. If possible, try to go to sleep at about the same time each night. This habit will make falling asleep much easier for the mind and body because it will allow your internal clock to become accustomed to a routine.

A common problem I know many people have is using electronic devices up until or even after they have gotten into bed. Your body needs time to shut down; otherwise you could find yourself tossing and turning for hours. The body naturally produces a hormone called Melatonin, which is regulated and affected by exposure to light. Melatonin aids in lowering your core body temperature, reducing the time it takes to fall asleep and in maintaining proper sleep cycles. Since Melatonin is regulated and affected by light, it is suggested to keep your sleeping environment as dark as possible, ideally to the point where you are unable to see your hand outstretched in front of your face. Continuously depriving yourself of a good night sleep will eventually lead to irritability, grogginess, and a weakened immune system. Give your mind and body enough sleep in order to continue functioning optimally each day.

Manage Your Finances Wisely

Many people do not understand the importance of having their finances in order. Disregarding time to put together a budget or a personal financial plan is one of the biggest mistakes a person can make. When you do not have a system in place to handle your money, you may find yourself living paycheck to paycheck, and leaving yourself vulnerable to make unwise decisions. This way of life leads to unwarranted spending instead of building a savings. It's never too early or too late in life to start saving money for your future. If you have trouble managing your money responsibly, look into finding a trustworthy financial advisor to take care of your investments and budgeting for you. Whether you want to put money away for a big investment such as a house or build a nest egg for your retirement, the sooner you start saving the better!

Making Time *For* You

Lastly, we cannot forget about making time for our mental and spiritual health. Whether you are a parent consumed by the chaos of raising a family or a student overwhelmed by your studies, you must find time for yourself to blow off some steam. Think of this time as "Me Time" and use it however you see fit to clear your mind, to analyze your growth, or to simply recharge. Sometimes you may want to read a book or go fishing, other times you may just need to find a quiet place to think and breathe. For me, my sanctuary is the beach. There is no place more calming to me than my favorite beach in Jupiter. I have been going to the same spot since I was in high school and I have many cherished memories there. Whether I go during the day or night, the sounds, smells, and scenery are enough to temporarily take away all of my troubles. When we don't take time to relieve stress, our anxiety levels elevate, our mind becomes clouded, and we may even begin to experience headaches, irritability, or exhaustion. Do not allow yourself to reach this point, start treating yourself to "Me Time" immediately.

We all live busy lives, some of us with schedules more hectic than others. But, it is imperative we do not use this as an excuse to make unhealthy decisions. Living a productive, healthy life requires time management, discipline, and the ability to make wise decisions when faced with more convenient alternatives that require less effort. It is easy to make choices that seem to offer a quick fix or grant us instant gratification. But it requires a trained mind to look at the big picture when it comes to making life decisions.

Part II: The Strength Within

Chapter 4: What It Takes to Succeed

"Put your heart, mind, and soul into even your smallest acts. This is the secret to success."

- Swami Sivananda

Every one of us has a different definition of "Success." For myself, I measure success by how many people I help during my lifetime. If I make a lot of money along the way, that's great, but that is not my primary motivator. Often, people ask me what I envision for my future and for the future of ZyckFit. Honestly, for myself, I will be content as long as I am able to provide for my family, friends, and still be able to enjoy life and give back to the less fortunate. My goals for the future include: training clients in my own gym, franchising my fitness boot camps, public speaking in a variety of settings, and making a positive impact on the world as often as possible. I see ZyckFit becoming a worldwide lifestyle brand synonymous with self-improvement and accomplishing goals. I would like to see people wearing ZyckFit apparel wherever I travel and have individuals using the hashtag "#ZyckFit" on social media to celebrate occasions such as their 10 year anniversary of being sober, getting their dream job, or hitting a new personal record in the gym. The potential for ZyckFit is limitless and I would like to see it develop into a movement that impacts as many lives as possible in a positive way!

Success does not come easy and it most certainly will not come overnight. The drive towards success must come from within, which requires being self-sufficient.

Regardless of how strong of a support system or team you have, it is imperative to be able to take care of things on your own. This requires discipline and self-confidence. You must believe wholeheartedly in your abilities and in your potential if you want to achieve your goals. If you can't count on yourself when the odds are stacked against you, then whom *can* you count on? Everyone has his or her own life and dreams to chase and, along the way, you need to be strong enough to be your own cheerleader and your biggest ally. Without confidence in yourself, no amount of help from others will make a difference.

Making Power Moves

Unfortunately, there is no magic formula or recipe for guaranteed success. It takes hard work, long hours, and sacrifice -- lots of sacrifice. To become successful, you must have your priorities in order, you have to surround yourself with the right people, and most importantly, you must have passion! Without passion, your dreams will be short lived and all of your hard work will be in vain. Besides the exception, if you are not happy with where you are in life, there is no one to blame except yourself. Staying in your comfort zone is not going to help you reach your goals. The sooner you realize this the better. In today's world, there are a number of ways to access resources and information free of charge, so what are you waiting for?

There is a great deal of negativity in the world and many people who will tell you that you cannot accomplish your goals. Fortunately, you do not have to prove yourself to anyone except yourself. This applies to every area in life. Strive to achieve greatness at school, at work, at home, and in everything you do. Achieve the physique you want, the job you want, the house you want, or whatever else it may be that you want in life. Figure out the steps it will take for you to get what you want, plan your strategy, then put in the work until you achieve results. Don't let injuries, prejudice, a lack of resources, a busy schedule, or anything else stop you!

This is your life and nobody else's. You have a limited time in this world and it should be spent doing the things you like to do. Spend your free time doing activities that make you happy, surround yourself with people that make you better, choose a career that you enjoy, and help inspire others to be the best they can be at every chance you get. Yes, life does throw curveballs at us sometimes, but just look at those as speed bumps. Although they may slow you down, never let them stop you. The only thing or person that can stop you from reaching your full potential is you!

You've heard the old adage "Where there's a will, there's a way." Throughout your lifetime, opportunities are not going to come to you, you have to go out and seek them yourself. I am a firm believer in the power of prayer, but prayer alone will not bring you what you are looking for. Prayer coupled with effort, however, can work wonders. If you want to make a connection with a certain person, make it happen. If you want to get a new job, make it happen. If you wait for opportunities to fall in your lap, you will most likely be waiting in vain. Good things don't always come to those who wait, but they do almost always come to those who work for them.

Looking At the Big Picture

Never give up when you are not seeing results as quickly as you would like. Trust the process; take baby steps if necessary. Anything worth having is worth fighting for: good grades in school, a rewarding career, a healthy body, etc. Most of the time, results do not come overnight. It takes discipline, consistency, and resilience to achieve your long-term goals, but it will all be worth it once you get there!

Always look at the big picture. At times, instant gratification, or a short-term solution may seem appealing, when in reality the long-term benefits and consequences must be considered as well. Looking at the big picture can be quite difficult when we are faced with offers or temptations that seem too good to be true. There are a number of documented examples of successful individuals in a variety of fields who turned down seemingly large sums of money because they knew in the long run their product or vision was worth much more. Have patience and weigh your options before making important decisions or taking action. If you can't think and plan long-term, don't expect long-term results.

Competition

There has been a growing sense of entitlement within our society in recent years. People seem to want to be handed things whether they worked for them or not. The "Everyone is a Winner" mindset is commonly used to avoid hurt feelings among children. On the contrary, this concept is hurting the same kids it is trying to protect. Children are not going to make every team they try out for, or win every award when they are young. To raise kids with a false sense of confidence is setting them up for a lifetime of heartbreak and discouragement. The truth is, it is OK to fail. We learn some of our greatest life lessons through failure and by making mistakes. Failure forces us to grow, adapt, and make changes. Entrepreneurship and the American Dream thrive on the idea of competition.

Competition forces an individual to improve. In nature, Darwinism states that you either adapt to your environment or outsmart your competition if you are to survive long enough to pass on your genes. I have been an extremely competitive person for as long as I can remember. In school, sports, and every day activities, I have always done my best to win or to be ahead of the curve. Average and "good enough" were never words I wanted used to describe me. When you hold yourself to a higher standard and have certain expectations, you give yourself a better shot at reaching your full potential. Allowing yourself to become stagnant or to settle for less will never get you anywhere in life. Even if you are only competing with yourself, find your competitive spirit and give life all you got! As singer Mick Jagger said, "Anything worth doing is worth overdoing."

Leaving Your Mark

"If you died tomorrow, how would you be remembered?" I ask myself this question often. We all like to think that we are good people and that we contribute to society, but how many of us *actually* make a lasting impact? I want to be a positive influence and leave a lasting legacy through my accomplishments and through my future children. Rather than how much money I make, I want my success in life to be measured by the number of lives I impact. Money comes and goes, but imparting wisdom on someone or changing a life is priceless.

So how do we go about leaving a lasting positive legacy? The legacy we leave is defined by our words, actions, and accomplishments while we are alive. Did we help others without expecting something in return? Did we honor our verbal agreements? Were we reliable and consistent in our commitments to others? When I die, I want the people I treated with kindness and selflessness to celebrate my life. As a Christian, I live my life embracing the ideas of Faith, Hope, and Charity. I try my best to treat others as I would like to be treated. An unknown author once said, "Live in such a way that if someone spoke badly of you, no one would believe it." I believe that is how one truly lives his or her life to the fullest, not by how many fancy possessions you amass over the years, but by the memories people have of you once you are gone.

Components of Success

The road to success can be extremely taxing on an individual. In order to accomplish all of your goals and live long enough to enjoy the rewards, it is essential to take care of your well-being. Everyone has at least one reason to live a healthy lifestyle: to become the best athlete possible, to look good, to prevent disease, or just to maintain functionality. While long-term goals are crucial, it helps to have a recurring idea or goal that you can review on a daily basis to reinforce why you are making sacrifices such as working out instead of being a couch potato, or putting money aside for your future instead of spending it on frivolous items. For me, I want to be better all around. Period. I want to be bigger, faster, stronger, and smarter. I never want to stop growing or learning. Many people reach a plateau or a comfort zone and then become content with their situation. As humans, we have so much potential to achieve greatness and we should be grateful every day that we have the opportunity to improve our lives! Determine your reasons for living a healthy lifestyle and what changes will be necessary to ensure lasting results. Remember, your health affects not only you, but also the lives of those around you. You will read more about how to develop a workout plan targeted specifically for you in a later chapter.

An individual can accomplish many great things alone, but so much more is possible with the help of others. Support systems, both personal and professional, provide resources and reassurance that are simply not available to someone trying to grow on their own. Expand your circle and open yourself up to a variety of people. Although it is good to be in the company of like-minded individuals, there is much to gain from others who think differently than you. When you meet new people, you open yourself up to fresh ideas and new experiences. This can lead to paths you had not previously considered exploring. We all know there is strength in numbers, with that being said, spend your time with the right people and you have a much better chance of becoming successful.

Mental and Spiritual alignment are paramount for success. Without these components, you will never find happiness in your lifetime. Mental and spiritual alignment will allow you to enjoy your place in life without having to compare yourself to anyone else or having to care about how society measures "success." Similar to how an athlete practices visualization before a game, you too must visualize what you are trying to accomplish in life. Attach a feeling to achieving that dream, and do not stop until you reach it. If you do not know your self-worth and believe in your dreams wholeheartedly, then you are not ready to begin your journey to success. Taking the time to get to know yourself is the most important investment you will ever make.

In conclusion, create your own definition of what it means to be successful. Never place boundaries on your dreams. There is nothing wrong with being unsure of your future or starting over. Failure is a part of life; learn from your mistakes and understand they are part of the growing process. Take care of your health, know what you want in life, surround yourself with genuine people, and believe deep down that your happiness is worth fighting for!

I Am ZyckFit: Tre's Story

You could say that I didn't grow up in the most favorable of conditions. I wasn't raised in the best neighborhood and role models were scarce. I grew up the hard way and I believe that contributes to why I am as tough as I am today. In addition to the non-traditional home life I was experiencing, school was never my strong suit. For me, street smarts have always come easier than book smarts. Shortly after the death of one of my uncles, my beloved mother passed away. Losing my mother at a young age definitely took a huge toll on me. That grief has always been with me and constantly reminds me that life is short. After the loss of my mother, my younger brother and I moved in with our father.

Unfortunately, I did not have the most supportive father, and after several bumpy years, he forced my brother and I to get out of his home. To say I never expected to find myself homeless would be an understatement. As I transitioned from job to job, trying to make ends meet, my living conditions were constantly changing and I never really felt at peace. To my surprise, my brother suddenly decided to leave the state to follow his own personal endeavors. As you can imagine, by this point, I was feeling abandoned, hopeless, and as if I was losing my faith.

I learned many lessons through my experiences during this period of time that made me the man I am today. I did what I had to do to survive without compromising my morals or integrity. One thing I have learned from ZyckFit is to *always* look for the good in every situation. I also learned that hard work and an insurmountable positive attitude can get you through anything.

Towards the end of 2015, I began working the front desk at Jupiter Fitness. It was at this time, that I met Tommy Rozycki. I immediately connected with Tommy and loved every thing he had planned for his company and his ideas to help change the world. Soon enough, Tommy and I became close friends, began working out together, and I became ZyckFit's first employee! Tommy has an infectious positive attitude and is full of wisdom that he is always more than willing to share with others.

Before ZyckFit, I was lacking direction in my life. And now, I believe in myself and feel more confident about my future than ever before! ZyckFit is more than just a fitness brand, it changes lives by changing the mind in a positive way. On top of everything our friendship has provided me with, I am most thankful to Tommy and ZyckFit for strengthening my relationship with God. Tommy is always the first one there to remind me that with prayer and faith, anything is possible!

"Be Better Today Than You Were Yesterday" should be the first thing you say to yourself when you wake up each morning. You should strive to be a better person every single day; whether that means you are attending a charity event to raise money for the less fortunate, supporting a good cause to make a better tomorrow for future generations, or even something as simple as holding the door for an older person. This is what being a better person today than you were yesterday means to me. Applying this mindset to my personal life reminds me to push myself just a little bit more every single day. With ZyckFit, I see more for my future than I ever have before!

Throughout life, every one of us is faced with countless trials and tribulations of varying degrees. Being on my own became more bearable once I began living the ZyckFit lifestyle. With the lessons I have learned from Tommy and ZyckFit, I have been able to endure the most difficult challenges I have faced so far in life. ZyckFit helped me get through them with a hopeful and refreshing outlook on life. I used to make my decisions in order to survive one day at a time, but ZyckFit taught me the importance of looking at the big picture and setting long-term goals. I used to look at life with a "You Only Live Once" attitude, but now I know I have to plan for my future if I want to become successful in life. ZyckFit taught me the importance of helping others and rejuvenated my faith in God! I am forever grateful for meeting Tommy and all he has done to help me improve myself mentally and physically which has led me to become a better person overall. I now realize I am worth more than I previously thought and my self-confidence will only grow from here!

Chapter 5: Who Are You?

"Happiness is not something ready made. It comes from your own actions."

- Dalai Lama

I chose to study Psychology in college for various personal reasons, but primarily because I have always been interested in human behavior. If you can understand how the human mind works, you will find yourself ahead of the curve in just about any situation in life. Being a student of Psychology allows me to modify my own behaviors as well as to understand the variety of behaviors and personalities I encounter every day.

Self-Actualization

Self-Actualization, the motivation to realize one's own maximum potential and possibilities, is one of the main components of ZyckFit. I believe it should be the goal of *every* human being to strive to become the best person they can be mentally, physically, and spiritually. Life is all about balance, and we must work towards achieving and maintaining this harmony between each of these components.

Self-Actualization doesn't happen for everyone. Most people live their entire life without realizing or reaching their full potential. An individual must *want* to better him or herself if a change is to occur. Self-Actualization is a lifelong process. We must constantly be learning and trying new things. You cannot grow if you do not challenge your way of thinking or living. It requires practice and discipline to recognize our weaknesses and to improve upon them. Your path to Self-Actualization will help you live a more purposeful, fulfilling life.

I first learned about Self-Actualization while studying Psychology in college. I have never been the type of person to settle for less than I think I deserve. If I want something in life, I figure out what it will take to achieve it, and then I keep trying until I get it. Sometimes, you have to be relentless to get what you want. I guess you can say I have an advantage over many people because I am naturally a competitive person and I have always enjoyed learning. These traits, along with being overtly stubborn, drive me to constantly want more out of life and expect more from myself. For example, I have improved my eating habits and work out almost every day. I have also begun reading every day again, attend church every week, have bank accounts for both savings and retirement, expand my social network whenever the opportunity arises, and do something every day to help ZyckFit grow. I know I am far from reaching my full potential, but I believe I am building the foundation for long-term success and happiness.

On your journey to Self-Actualization, take time each day to reflect on where you are and where you want to be in life. Be honest with yourself and understand that you have much more learning and growing to do regardless of your age, profession, or status. We each have our own path in life and we should all aim to become the best versions of ourselves.

Self-Talk

Self-talk is the way you communicate ideas about yourself, both internally and externally. Self-talk can either be positive or negative. The mindset you have approaching a situation (a workout, a date, a job interview, etc.) will make all the difference on the outcome because confidence, or lack thereof, can be one of your greatest assets or one of your greatest downfalls. When we use negative self-talk we are inadvertently sabotaging ourselves with doubt. Fortunately, it *is* possible to consciously improve the way we think about ourselves. The first step you should take is removing the word "can't" from your vocabulary. Next, anytime you find yourself using counter-productive or inflammatory self-talk, replace those thoughts with positive, reinforcing thoughts. It may seem silly or impossible at first, but if you keep at it persistently, you *can* change the way you think about yourself.

Choose Happiness

We all have different things in life that make us happy. In today's society, happiness is usually tied to wealth and fancy possessions. Money may make certain things in life easier, but it certainly cannot buy happiness. Money comes and goes, but you can't take it with you once you are gone. I met some of the happiest, kindest individuals I have ever known at the mental health clinic where I worked; individuals with no money, who suffered from severe mental illnesses, and who have lived through a number of horrible life experiences. Regardless of what they were going through in their own lives, these people would go out of their way to brighten someone's day if they noticed he or she was in a bad mood or if something was wrong. Many of them relied on their faith to stay positive; while others simply understood the fact that waking up every day with a negative mindset was not going to make things any better. Former NFL coach Lou Holtz said, "Life is ten percent what happens to you and ninety percent how you respond to it." We have a choice every single day when we wake up regarding how we want to face the world: we can either sulk in our misery and blame others for our misfortunes or we can look for the good in every situation and help spread positivity to others who may need it more than us. Count your blessings, because there is always someone worse off than you. Life is short, and if your happiness depends on material possessions, you will never be truly satisfied with what you have.

For me, true happiness comes from my relationship with God, time spent with loved ones, and the satisfaction that comes from helping others. My faith has become my rock and it allows me to take away at least one positive lesson from every situation. It is important to surround yourself with positive people -- individuals with ambition, who believe in you, and who want to see you succeed. There are many toxic people in the world who want to see you fail or for you to remain stagnant. Some of these individuals have been in your life for years, and although it may be tough, it is best for you, in the long run, to cut them out of your life. Whether it is your personal or professional life, a strong, dependable support system is crucial for success and happiness. A good team around you can help you reach your goals much faster than you would on your own. To me, making memories with family and friends is more valuable than any amount of money in the world. Good memories and relationships last forever and can keep you going even through the toughest times.

Throughout life we are faced with adversities and tough decisions that cause both physical discomfort and mental turmoil; personal issues, financial problems, and worldly troubles to name a few. Finding one or more healthy outlets from stress is essential to living a happy and enjoyable life. Surrounding yourself with positive, goal-oriented individuals is a great way to get your mind off of something bothering you or even to help you solve the problem permanently. Having someone to talk to, especially someone who can relate to what you are going through, is one of the most effective ways of dealing with stress. Nobody can tell you who you are, but others can help you discover more about yourself. Sometimes our loved ones and the people we spend the most time with see things that we are unable to see for ourselves. Their perspective can be invaluable in your quest for self-improvement.

No one is perfect, and even though I strive to be the best I can be, I have suffered from mild anxiety for as long as I can remember. It is a constant feeling and tends to intensify during certain situations. My anxiety is a part of who I am. Although my anxiety can hinder me, I also see it as an asset at times. Arriving to places early, being attentive to details, both traits I attribute to my anxiety, have helped me throughout the years academically, socially, and professionally. The takeaway from this is to always look for blessings, even when something may seem like a curse.

Know Yourself

We are all put on this Earth for a reason, and it is up to each of us to figure out what that reason is. Some people are teachers, some are entertainers, others are warriors or healers; finding your purpose in the world is one of the most important parts of life. We are all blessed with at least one "gift" or ability, and discovering what that talent is takes time, introspection, and life experiences. Set time aside to learn more about yourself; you will become better, smarter, and more efficient if you do. Once you are aware of your gift(s), it is your responsibility to utilize them and share them with the world. Along the way, help others develop their own gifts; you never know what you may learn in the process.

Who are you? I am talking about the person deep down on the inside; the real you regardless of who is around. What do you stand for? Which of your values are uncompromising? Are you living your life for yourself or for someone else's approval? If you don't regularly make time to take inventory of your inner-self, then you are robbing yourself of potential growth. If you are not in touch with who you are, then you will never find true happiness because you don't even know what you are searching for. I believe most people are afraid to openly be themselves because they are not sure other people will approve of who they really are on the inside. So, instead, they act against what feels natural in order to be accepted. Let me tell you this, that is not living and if you know people like that, they are not the right people for you. We are each granted a God-given personality for a reason and it takes all types of people to make the world go round. That being said, never be afraid to be yourself!

I understand the question "Who are you?" will not be answered by the time you finish reading this book, but I hope a spark has been ignited in your mind to begin learning more about yourself. To be honest, discovering who we are is a lifelong process because we are constantly changing due to our environment, interactions, and experiences. Take time at the end of each day to review what you learned or experienced in order to prepare for your future. When you are well-prepared in life, regardless of the situation, you have a much better chance of succeeding.

I Am ZyckFit: R.B.'s Story

In order to maintain his professional integrity, a good friend of mine asked to remain anonymous. Here is his story:

How do I begin? Where do I start? What is my purpose? These are questions I have always asked myself but have never seemed to be able to figure out in life. At the time of writing this, I am 26 years old and I honestly did not "find" myself until about three years ago.

I grew up in a neighborhood in a small city outside of Frankfurt, Germany, where most youngsters feel pressured to be as tough or as naïve, you could say, as the "big city" kids. In school, we had more fights than classes in a day, drug deals were common, and teachers lived in fear half of the time. Although I was raised in a good household, the neighborhood made my childhood a total roller coaster. Growing up, I had everything a child needed: good parents, a roof over my head, and plenty to eat. We never struggled and I can't say that I ever had to steal to survive or worry where my next meal was coming from. But shortly after my parents broke up when I was around 10 years old, I started to surround myself with people that turned my life for the worse.

I smoked my first joint when I was 11 years old and I first experienced alcohol poisoning when I was 12. Between the ages of 14-16, I sold more drugs at school and the neighborhood park than the average kid eats candy. I even robbed other drug dealers at gunpoint occasionally. The first time I was arrested was at age

15 for severely breaking somebody's face. Fortunately for me, Germany's justice system is lenient towards minors, and after serving my community service hours, I was off the hook. At the time, I couldn't comprehend the damage I was causing my family or myself. My crew had become the biggest and baddest around, so life was good right? Well the truth is, slowly but surely, more and more of the people around me were either being deported to their home countries, arrested, or becoming untrustworthy.

Eventually, my crew shrank to a small circle of reliable friends I considered brothers. Change, whether good or bad, is guaranteed in life. This is one of the first lessons I learned in my youth. Here I was at 17 years old, about to graduate high school, a feat that still surprises me to this day. I had no perspective, no job, and no direction in life. Soon enough, I had stopped doing drugs and couldn't remember the last time I was in a fight or committed a crime. At home one day, I received a phone call that changed my life. It was my father. He had been living in the United States for about 7 years in Richmond, Virginia. He asked me if I would be interested in moving to the U.S., because I was born as an American citizen, and attend college. This took me as a surprise since I had never been the best student in the past. I saw it as an opportunity to change my life for the better and to prove to everyone who didn't believe in me that I could be successful! On August 27th 2008, twenty days after my eighteenth birthday, I flew to "the Land of Opportunity"-- the United States of America!

Three months later, I was improving my English, working a job washing dishes, and preparing to begin school at a community college. I still had this drive to prove to the world that I would "be better today than I was yesterday"-- #ZyckFit. I graduated with my Associate's Degree with a 3.8 GPA and began applying to schools in Florida because I would soon be moving there with my family. After touring several campuses, I decided to attend the best university in ALL of Florida: the University of Central Florida. Although I was relatively successful in school, I still found myself falling back into old patterns from my past. Two of the biggest issues I had were that I could not fully trust anyone and I was also lying a lot. I met many good people in college, and I was very fortunate to meet Tommy Rozycki.

At first, Tommy and I didn't hit it off, mostly because we didn't share a lot of the same friends. However, after a while we ran into each other more often and slowly became good friends. One of the first things that stood out with Tommy was that he cares a lot about people and he is also very honest. I believe it has a lot to do with his faith in God and the great relationship he has with his parents. Both of his parents are honest and caring people just like Tommy, and I am very lucky to have had the privilege of meeting them! If there is one thing I can tell you about Tommy Rozycki, it would be that long before he had the idea of starting his own company, he was already trying to help others live a happier, healthier lifestyle, and to empower people to never stop improving. Tommy acted as the backbone for many people and he never expected or rarely received any kind of recognition. Yes, I have seen him fail multiple times, but I have also seen him get right back up again and again. If there was anyone out there to look up to when it came to having a positive mindset, it was Tommy Rozycki! Tommy personally helped me improve my life in so many ways. During the times when I was unsure of myself or uncertain about what was next for me, he supported me. I am happy to call Tommy more than just a friend. Because of him, I now have faith in people and learned to trust others again.

About a year after I met Tommy, I met my beautiful wife. I owe a lot of gratitude to her as well. With her, I learned to love, forgive, and be loyal again. If you surround yourself with the right people that you can trust, there is no limit to what you can accomplish together. Nothing in life is handed to you and you should never take things for granted. I have learned to appreciate those around me who truly support me.

I am always looking for new ways to be better today than I was yesterday! To this day, I still can't believe how far I have come in the past 10 years. Today, I am a father and a husband; I have a successful career, and a long, happy life ahead of me. I have proved to those who didn't believe in me that I DID IT!

Regardless of what happens in life, if you have the will do something, there is a way to accomplish it. To me, ZyckFit means having faith in yourself and working hard every day for your dreams. It is more than just getting up in the morning and knowing what you need to accomplish. ZyckFit means giving 110% every day to make your dreams come true! There is always room for improvement on a day-to-day basis. If you have the right attitude and mindset, anything in life is possible! Trust me, you can '"be better today than you were yesterday!"'

Chapter 6: What Drives You?

"If you are interested, you'll do what's convenient. If you are committed, you'll do what it takes."

\- John Assaraf

The motivation behind the desire to be successful is different for everyone. Money, fame, and security are a few examples of why people dedicate so much of their time and effort to becoming successful. Personally, there are several motives behind my desire to succeed: the satisfaction of helping my family and friends, the work ethic bestowed upon me by my parents, innate ambition to be the best I can be and, above all else, a calling from God to help as many people as possible.

I wake up every day genuinely excited to improve myself and to also help as many people as I can. As mentioned in Chapter 1, I believe that total health requires a balance of mind, body, and soul. I exercise to be strong physically, I read to be strong mentally, and I pray to be strong spiritually. I am grateful that God constantly challenges me to be the best I can be and that He also presents me with countless opportunities to help me better my life. I attribute everything that is good about myself to God and to my faith. My health, intelligence, and athleticism were all given to me by God, and it is up to me to work hard to improve what I have been entrusted with. I do not take anything I have for granted and I always push myself 100% for whatever it is I am working towards. I am confident that I will be successful in reaching more and more people in the years to come with ZyckFit because I truly believe that is God's plan for me!

Whatever your belief system may be, always try to spread positivity, not only to your loved ones, but also to the people you encounter in your daily life. Always be kind, because you never know what battles or troubles the individuals around you are struggling with each day. Use your abilities and gifts for the greater good. With a little effort every day, each one of us can make a difference in the world. American author and political activist, Helen Keller, said, "Alone we can do so little; together we can do so much." Make it a goal to help someone each and every day!

Why I Do What I Do

Besides helping others, nothing in my life makes me happier than spending time with my family and friends. My support system consists of good-hearted, driven individuals who genuinely care about my future. Some friends I have known for a couple of decades, while others I have met only over the past few years, yet they have already become a huge part of my life. The people we interact with on a daily basis, the ones we invest our time and emotions into, impact us in a number of ways. Spending quality time with loved ones and those that are positive influences is good for us physically, mentally, and emotionally. Do your best to remove toxic individuals from your life who are not contributing anything worthwhile to your future. As painful as this may be, it is necessary if you are to flourish and grow to your full potential.

From a young age, I have admired the work ethic and character of my parents and grandmother. I was raised to respect others, work hard for what I want in life, and stand up for what I believe in. My family has provided me with so much over the years. This is why I work hard every day -- so I can attempt to repay them for all that they have done for me. I hope they are proud of the man I am becoming and all that I have accomplished thus far in my life. Making my family proud helped me avoid making poor decisions growing up and remain an honor roll student throughout my academic career. Are you making choices on a daily basis that your loved ones can be proud of? Learn to listen to and take criticism from those around you. You can learn more about yourself this way than you can solely on your own.

Although I do not have children yet, I pray that I do become a father someday. And the responsibility of raising a family is an important motivating factor for me. I always try to think long-term, and raising my kids comfortably is already on my mind. I plan to reach a level of success where I am able to put away enough money to take care of any expected and unexpected expenses in their lives. Don't get me wrong, my kids *will* work for many things on their own, but their security is still an important motivating factor for me, even at this point in my life.

Ambition is defined as "a strong desire to do or to achieve something, typically requiring determination and hard work."

Ambition wakes you up in the morning ready to go and pushes you to work relentlessly towards your dreams every day until you are ready for bed each night. I think certain individuals have an intrinsic sense of ambition, but I also believe ambition can be learned. If you do not consider yourself a "go-getter", choose positive role models you can learn from, surround yourself with driven individuals, and train yourself to become more productive through time management, goal setting, and self-discipline. Read motivational books, watch inspirational videos, and create systems that allow you to use your time more efficiently. Without ambition, you are settling for whatever life hands you instead of creating your own future.

Similar to ambition, I believe work ethic is learned and can be improved upon. Sadly, many people are content with being ordinary. By this, I mean they are satisfied with waking up every day, going to work, going home, and repeating the same process year after year without attempting to make any life changes. Furthermore, most people are not willing to see how much productivity they can squeeze into each day. A solid work ethic will demonstrate that you are reliable and responsible. People will support and cheer for someone that is genuine and determined in their effort to become successful. Put solid effort into everything you do, and the results will follow.

If you believe, or if someone else has told you, that your work ethic can be improved upon, it is time to re-evaluate your priorities. If you procrastinate often or habitually put your responsibilities low on your To-Do list, it is time to make some changes. Create a schedule to make the most of every week, set goals to avoid distractions, and actively look for opportunities to improve your life on a daily basis. At school and work, consistently give each assignment or customer your full attention, and always be honest in your work. These qualities will get you far, not only in academics and in your career, but also in life!

During college, I attended classes, played intramural sports, was a member of a dance crew, and maintained an active social life. After graduating, I worked multiple jobs simultaneously including: car valet, pizza delivery, and medical assistant. These jobs required long hours, early mornings, and late nights. When you want to be successful, you will do whatever it takes to get there. I always reminded myself that my situation was temporary, those jobs were stepping stones, and I was still far from being where I wanted to be in life. These reminders kept me from becoming stagnant and settling for less than I knew I deserved. Although I knew those jobs were only temporary, I still worked hard every day and provided the best customer service possible at all times. I learned much about myself during those years. Above all else, though, I learned how far I am willing to push my mind and body in order to succeed. If you want your dreams to come true, you have to be willing to do whatever it takes for however long it takes until those dreams become a reality.

Selflessness

Helping others is what ZyckFit and my life are all about. I believe selflessness is one of the greatest signs of strength in a person's character. Writer and preacher, John Bunyan, said, "You have not lived today until you have done something for someone who can never repay you." When we assist others without looking for recognition or something in return, we not only help that individual, we also inadvertently help ourselves become better as well. I try my hardest every day to remain selfless in my thoughts and in my actions so that I am able to improve the lives of those around me. Every career path I have ever been passionate about (teacher, therapist, trainer) has been focused on helping others become the best they can be. Are your priorities self-centered or selfless? Take time to analyze *why* you do the things you do and who they are impacting.

Live Life On Your Terms

One of my greatest fears in life is being "average" or "ordinary". The thought of reaching the end of my life and looking back with regrets or having a feeling of dissatisfaction frightens me. Life is short and the world is a big place with many places to see and tons of people to meet. Why not try your hardest to do everything you want to do while you still have the chance? I want to make a name for myself and for my future children that is respected and known around the world for helping others. I do not want my life to pass me by without accomplishing all of my goals, travelling the world, and impacting as many lives with positivity as possible. I believe every person should live his or her life to the fullest. You never know what opportunities await you outside of your comfort zone!

Every person has an ideal lifestyle he or she wants to achieve one day. Some people seek a big house and fancy cars, some want to travel the world, while others are content with living a more simple life. Whatever type of lifestyle you envision for yourself, you can achieve it if you believe in yourself. Every dream begins with a *desire* -- a motivating force to become a famous actor, a star athlete, a powerful CEO, or even the best mother or father possible. Unfortunately, desire is not enough to make a dream come true. Dreams are made possible through persistence, sacrifice, self-belief, and hard work. A dream will remain just that, a dream, unless you are willing to do what is necessary to make it a reality.

How Strong Is Your "Why?"

Why are you going back to school? Why do you work two jobs? Why haven't you given up yet? Whatever your motivating force(s) are, they must be present with you every single day, especially on the days you feel like giving up. Your "Why?" has to be strong enough to get you through the toughest days when you are struggling or feeling lazy. Every day is a gift and should be treated like one. Do not take anything you have for granted. Ask yourself who or what matters the most in your life and how hard you are willing to work for them. With the right attitude, you can be unstoppable.

If your dreams do not scare you, then perhaps they simply are not big enough. Whether it requires a higher education, countless hours on the field, or financial discipline, success and fulfilling your dreams will only come after sacrifices are made. Dreams are powerful ideas because they can get you through even the toughest times. Many successful people in the world have overcome poverty, homelessness, and a number of other obstacles thanks to their inner drive to be better. Remember, the only person who can place limitations on your dreams is you.

Believe in yourself, work hard, never say never, and above all else, do not allow your **dreams to** die. If you give up on your dreams, you will never know how truly happy you could have been in life!

I Am ZyckFit: Nancy's Story

Throughout my adult years, I have always worked out at a gym. But a few years ago, I suffered a ruptured disc in my lower back, which kept me from exercising for quite some time. And by age 62, I found myself fifteen pounds overweight and in need of a change. I decided it was time to return to the gym with high hopes of getting back into shape and dropping the weight.

Quite fearful of damaging my back, I took it slow as I gradually eased back into my workouts. As you can probably guess, this led to zero results. Then I noticed one of the senior fitness classes happening at the gym and thought to myself that might be what I needed. I mentioned this to my husband who suggested I try a personal trainer who could safely and skillfully get me back on track.

After a disappointing and frustrating experience with a personal trainer nearly two decades ago, I was apprehensive about turning to another one for help. But, after the encouraging words of my better half, I decided to try again.

Then, Tommy Rozycki came into my life. During our first meeting, he patiently listened to the limitations I had imposed on myself. Tommy then put together a plan to fit my needs. As I progressed, I became more confident in his knowledge and skills. And as my strength returned, my attitude became more positive and my energy soared! Tommy believed in me so much, even when I did not believe in myself, and I became determined to not let him down. My goals were to work harder and make every minute under his care count. I totally trusted Tommy.

The defining factor for my weight loss journey was a "Before and After" picture that Tommy posted online of his transformation toward his goal of gaining 15 pounds. After seeing his progress, I was struck with the idea of just how much control we have over how our bodies can look and feel. Tommy stated a goal and achieved it. That is an important component of ZyckFit -- setting goals and working hard until you accomplish them. From that moment on, I took control too. I lost the 15 pounds I desired and built some lean muscle as well. It was an amazing feeling!

I am now free of back pain and I no longer have reservations about working out hard. I love the feeling of strength and confidence I discovered while training with ZyckFit. Tommy has had an incredibly positive influence on me and I applaud him for his dedication to help people become healthy. With that, comes happiness and strength inside and out!

In addition to improving my fitness, I have gained much more since being introduced to ZyckFit. Having experienced my sister's untimely death in late 2015, ZyckFit brought me through the grief without turning to and relying on medications. A training session with Tommy was always enough to chase away the stress and negative emotions I was feeling. ZyckFit became a lifeline for me during those dark times, and training multiple times a week with Tommy helped me maintain my sanity. Instead of taking medications to numb the pain, our training sessions would send me home feeling fifteen years younger, energetic, and brimming with happiness!

ZyckFit has been a life changing experience for me, as I learned to take control of my fitness again and reap the rewards of being healthy and active every day. There isn't a pill in the world that could do that. ZyckFit did it for me!

Part III: Building a Better You!

Chapter 7: Nutrition

"The wise man should consider that health is the greatest of human blessings. Let food be your medicine."

- Hippocrates

Now that you are motivated to make a change, it is time to begin building a better you! A healthy body and mind begins with proper nutrition.

For me, food was not always my friend. Don't get me wrong, I have always enjoyed eating, just not in the same way most people do. For the majority of my life, I suffered from terrible anxiety whenever faced with trying new foods. If I was not comfortable with the appearance, smell, taste, or texture, there was no way I was trying it. This anxiety was so great, it affected me in multiple aspects of my life: physically, mentally, socially, and emotionally. When I *could* actually work up the nerve to try a new food, more often than not, I would get physically repulsed and gag or spit it out almost immediately. I missed out on countless social events growing up because I knew what would happen if there wasn't food I was comfortable with to choose from. I grew up lying to friends that I couldn't sleep over their houses or attend their birthday parties due to my issues with food. There have been numerous times where I have been hungry and told someone I didn't feel like eating in order to save myself the embarrassment. Other times, I would fill up on comfort foods before arrival so I wouldn't have to go without eating for the duration of the event. Living like this led to feelings of embarrassment, inadequacy, and shame. I developed an inferiority complex and kept my secret from even my closest friends for years.

I know most people cannot relate and will not understand where I am coming from, but we all have our own personal battles and this was mine for years. I sought help from doctors and therapists, but deep down I always knew it was a problem I would have to overcome on my own.

Eventually, armed with methods I learned from studying Psychology in school and a strong support system of family and friends, I slowly began leaving my comfort zone and expanding my variety of foods, finally giving my body the proper nourishment it deserved. Before college, I had never eaten a fruit, vegetable, or any type of meat. The only source of protein I had ever received was from dairy products. In high school, my bodyweight could not surpass 165 pounds, but as I increased my protein intake in college, I quickly shot up to 178 pounds. Although I am still not a fearless eater, and I may never be, my eating habits have improved dramatically and that will only continue to improve throughout my life!

I believe there is something good to be taken from every situation in life. Although I struggled with this eating problem for many years, it helped shape the person I am today. It taught me to understand that we are all unique in our own ways and that you never truly know what someone else is going through. I am grateful that my problem is a relatively minor one compared to the number of addictions, illnesses, and afflictions that others suffer from every day. My eating habits were the main reason I studied Psychology in college as well as the reason I have worked so hard to remain active during my lifetime. I could have let my anxiety and discomfort damage my self-esteem and my social life but, instead, I decided to make the changes necessary to enjoy my life the way I want.

Then, for several years after college, I found it nearly impossible to gain weight once again. No matter how much I worked out, I remained around 178 pounds. I believed I was eating enough food and brushed off advice from friends and co-workers who told me otherwise. But, in an effort to make a change, at the end of 2015, I set a goal to gain more lean muscle mass. I began eating more meals on a daily basis; most of the time when I was not even hungry. In addition to eating more, I started regularly drinking three protein shakes a day as opposed to just one after my workout. It turns out, the people around me were right, because after I combined these nutritional changes with my existing workout routine, my weight increased to 195 pounds in just a few months. Take my word for it, the solution to reaching your fitness and wellness goals is changing your eating habits. Whether you want to lose weight, put on muscle, or just feel better in general, what you eat, how often you eat, and how much you eat will make all the difference.

The importance of nutrition cannot be emphasized enough. What you put into your body is the fuel that keeps every cell, muscle, and organ functioning properly. It really is true that you cannot outwork a bad diet. No matter how hard or how often you exercise, if you do not have the proper eating habits, you will never achieve the physique you desire. An unhealthy diet sabotages all of the hard work you endure while exercising. Not only is an unhealthy diet counterproductive to your workouts, it also affects your mood and energy level. Remember: eat well, look good, feel good!

A balanced diet is the framework for a healthy lifestyle. Without proper nutrition, your body will be unable to function and perform at its best. Think of your body like a car; you must put the best fuel into it if you expect it to work efficiently for years to come. Nowadays, there are a number of opinions on what foods should and should not be consumed. There are concerns about GMOs and other additives among our food supply. Some people eat strictly organic, some are Paleo, some avoid Gluten, and others stick to the basics they have always thought to be acceptable to eat. Every person has his or her own preferences, dislikes, and restrictions. A healthy diet consists of a balance of lean proteins such as chicken and fish, good carbohydrates from sources like vegetables and rice, and good fats including almonds and avocados.

Depending on your goals and your quality of life, your diet may be more or less lenient than others. Moderation and smart choices are key when indulging or straying from your usual routine. One rule of thumb which is undeniable regardless of one's eating habits is that portion control is imperative. It is not a good idea to eat to the point where you become uncomfortably full. This will only lead to excess calories, bloating, and a feeling of sluggishness. This may seem obvious to some, but "finishing your plate" and not letting food "go to waste" are common themes in many households, but this mindset can actually be harmful. Meal planning is an effective tool to avoid overeating. Measure portions for each meal you will be eating during the week to make sure you will eat enough and that no food will be wasted. Listen to your body, do your research, and practice sound judgment when shopping, cooking, and dining out.

Supplements

Although food is the most effective and natural method of receiving nutrients, at times, we require additional supplements and vitamins to make up for what is missing from our diet. Not only are supplements important for complimenting our diets, they are also important for boosting the immune system and aiding the organs in functioning properly. At the very least, it is wise to take a once a day multi-vitamin to guarantee you are receiving an adequate amount of vitamins and minerals. Be sure to research any supplements and vitamins before adding them to your health regimen.

Hydration

The human body is composed of approximately 60% water. Therefore, it is essential to stay adequately hydrated throughout the day. A few signs of dehydration include headache, dry skin, and fatigue. Because I grew up and played sports in South Florida, I understand hydration is of great importance for safety, health, and performance. Carry a water bottle with you to school, work, and the gym so you are constantly reminded to hydrate. Substitute water instead of juices and sodas to eliminate extra calories and sugar intake from your diet. If you do not enjoy drinking water, try a garnish such as a lime or cucumber to improve the flavor. Whatever works for you, be sure to drink a minimum of 8 glasses of water a day, and even more if you live an active lifestyle.

Metabolism

A fast metabolism is important in achieving and maintaining a healthy weight. Several factors affect your metabolism including your age, activity level, and hormones. The key to revving up your metabolism is a *variety* in your diet and in your workouts. A common misconception is that you burn most of your calories while exercising, when in fact your Resting Metabolic Rate (RMR) accounts for 70% of your total daily caloric expenditure. Your RMR is the rate at which your body burns calories throughout the day, even when you are at rest (sleeping, watching TV, working, etc.) It is a proven fact that lean muscle burns more calories than fat does. According to the American Council on Exercise, on average, muscle burns 7-10 calories/lb each day while fat only burns 2-3 calories/lb a day. Therefore, it is important to decrease your total body fat and to increase your lean muscle mass. You can accomplish this through consistency with exercise and proper nutrition.

Several factors which can have a negative impact on your metabolism include age, skipped meals, hormones, medications, stress, and lack of sleep. Unfortunately, some of these factors are out of our control, but like many things in life, we have to make the best of what we *do* have control over. Stay consistent with your workouts, eat a healthy diet, find activities to relieve stress, and get the rest your body needs.

Digestive Health

Neglecting your digestive health can lead to discomfort and a number of complications including indigestion, acid reflux, constipation, and bloating. Staying hydrated, getting adequate sleep, exercising, and avoiding overeating are habits you can incorporate into your daily routine to improve your digestion. Take your time when you eat and avoid foods that do not agree with your stomach. Two additional ways of aiding your digestive system are increasing your fiber intake and consuming Probiotics.

Fiber is an important component of a balanced diet. It is recommended that you aim for approximately 25-30 grams of fiber in your diet every day. This number can be reached by eating fruits, vegetables, and grains. There are two main types of dietary fiber: soluble and insoluble. Foods high in soluble fiber leave you feeling full longer by delaying the emptying of the stomach. Soluble fibers can have a positive effect on weight loss, Diabetes, and bad cholesterol. Oatmeal, apples, and nuts are a few of the foods containing soluble fiber. Insoluble fiber does not dissolve in water and stays almost completely intact throughout the entire digestive process. Insoluble fiber is also beneficial for weight loss as well as for preventing conditions including constipation and Diverticulitis. Quality sources of insoluble fiber include, but are not limited to, broccoli, tomatoes, corn, and whole grains.

In addition to fiber, Probiotics are another means for improving your digestion. Probiotics are live microorganisms that are believed to be great for digestive health, help boost the immune system, decrease pathogens, and improve bowel regularity. You can either get your recommended dosage of Probiotics, at least 1-2 million CFUs (Colony-Forming Units), from food or from supplements. Probiotics help balance the "good" and "bad" bacteria to keep your body functioning properly. Yogurt, milk, and cheese are all natural sources of Probiotics.

Caffeine

It is well known that caffeine is the most commonly used drug in the world. Caffeine can be found in varying amounts inside foods, beverages, and medications. According to a study by New Scientist magazine, 90% of North American adults consume some form of caffeine on a daily basis. Caffeine offers benefits ranging from increased energy to improved memory and alertness. Caffeine helps people get their day started, keeps employees awake at work, and aids students in staying focused while studying. However, over time, your body can become physically dependent on caffeine and may suffer from withdrawal symptoms such as headaches, irritability, and anxiety if consumption is reduced or eliminated.

Sadly, society has become infatuated with caffeine consumption. Any day of the week, you can find a person leaving the grocery store with a shopping cart full of soda bottles or see a long line of people out the door at the nearest Starbucks waiting to get their hands on a coffee topped with whipped cream, caramel, and other fattening additives. There is nothing wrong with an occasional treat, but drinking these beverages on a daily basis will slowly add up on your waistline and have a negative effect on your health. I personally do not drink coffee, but I do try to drink at least one cup of green tea every day. Green tea provides powerful antioxidants as well as improves brain and heart health. Green tea is also a great alternative to water when trying to avoid drinking sodas, juices, and alcoholic beverages. Caffeinated, sugary drinks are popular among kids but should be limited or eliminated to avoid bad habits and an early onset of weight gain.

Childhood Obesity

According to the CDC, Childhood Obesity has more than doubled in children and quadrupled in adolescents in the past 30 years. That is an alarmingly frightening statistic. Childhood Obesity can mainly be attributed to unhealthy eating habits and a sedentary lifestyle. In addition to the negative physical side effects, weight gain can have a harmful impact on a child's self-esteem and confidence.

Poor nutrition is the largest and fastest contributor to weight gain. Every day, kids are tricked into wanting junk food due to exposure to numerous TV commercials, colorful food packages, and fun cartoon characters. It is the parents' job to instill good eating habits into the minds of their children. Adults control what is brought into the house from the grocery store and they decide how often the family goes out to eat. Although many restaurants now offer healthier options, cooking at home will always be the best way to monitor the portions and ingredients your family is consuming. School cafeterias tend to offer cheap, low-quality food options and unhealthy products from large franchises to their students. This is why it is best to prepare your children's lunches at home. Your children are relying on you, not only for proper nutrition, but for proper education as well. Children will model whatever behavior they observe, so make sure you are setting a good example.

In this age of ever-growing technology, some may argue that children are less active than ever before. We need to get back to the days when kids used their imaginations instead of iPads. Technology has become a babysitter causing kids to no longer feel the need to go outside to have fun. Teach your children to exercise while they are young and this may very well increase the chances of them staying active throughout their lives. Physical activity among children aids in proper growth and development, as well as improved motor skills and coordination. Enroll your kids in a camp or register them to play on a sports team. During the summer, bring them to the beach or pool and increase water intake to avoid dehydration and heat exhaustion. Keep exercising fun and engaging to avoid boredom and disinterest. Set up play dates with other parents so your children can make new friends. Designate a short block of time each day for your kids to be allowed to play video games and watch TV, otherwise they should be doing something more productive. At the very least, make sure your kids get the suggested 30 minutes of exercise each day. The health and future of our children are in our hands and we must show them the correct way to eat and exercise!

For some, going to the gym and eating right every day comes naturally, while for others, being disciplined in regard to exercise and clean eating takes work. That is why this is *your* journey. A healthy lifestyle requires a balance of both exercise and nutrition, so it is important to make them both priorities. Now that you know the importance of nutrition, it is time to develop a workout program that works for you!

Chapter 8: Create Your Workout Program

"To keep the body in good health is a duty. Otherwise, we shall not be able to keep our mind strong and clear."

- Buddha

Before you begin creating a workout plan that works for you, let's get to know a little about the body's main muscle groups. When it comes to exercising, there are six primary muscle groups to be trained: Chest, Back, Arms, Shoulders, Legs, and Abs.

It is important to incorporate a balance of all six muscle groups in your workout routine. A proportionate body is essential to avoid muscle imbalance, maintain proper mechanics, and ensure good posture. It is never a good idea to neglect any of the major muscle groups.

Our upper body is used on a daily basis for a variety of functions and must remain strong and durable in order to avoid wear and tear or debilitation. The Chest, Back, Arms, and Shoulders can be trained separately or in various combinations depending on preference. Your core muscles (Abs) are responsible for stability and balance in just about every exercise, sport, and activity. A strong core also helps to prevent or improve lower back pain. It is important to keep the lower body strong in order to maintain a lifetime of mobility and functionality. Whether you are a seasoned athlete or just exercise to remain active, keeping your Legs strong throughout your life may keep you from being bound to a wheelchair or bed in your later years.

Your Workout Program

Now that you are more familiar with the body's muscle groups, it is time for you to create a workout plan that is geared specifically for *you*! It is important that you enjoy your workouts or else it is less likely you will continue to exercise regularly for years to come. Remember, you are exercising to improve your long-term quality of life. Working out is not meant to be a chore or a form of torture. Exercise and nutrition are a lifetime commitment and should be enjoyable.

The amount of time you dedicate to exercising each week depends on your schedule and goals. A young, hungry athlete is going to spend hours upon hours improving his or her skills, while an older man or woman may be satisfied with going for a daily walk or bike ride. Thirty minutes of daily moderate to vigorous physical activity is the recommended minimum but can be and should be increased if you are able to or have ambitious goals. Some people prefer working out 2-3 times per week, while other individuals like to exercise every day. All that matters is that you avoid a sedentary lifestyle and that you find ways of exercising that you enjoy!

There are a number of approaches you can take to design your workout program and it is a good idea to make changes to it every so often. Some athletes prefer full-body workouts, while others focus on targeting specific muscle groups each session.

And it is important to recognize that you may be limited to which exercises you are able to perform due to age, injury, or ability.

If you have an injury or condition that limits your physical capabilities, there is usually a way to modify an activity so you are able to perform it. In Yoga, there are easier positions for stretching. In gyms, there is a variety of machines or exercises to compensate for handicaps or limitations. There is no shame in doing things at a slower pace or at a lower intensity than others. As long as you are challenging yourself, you are improving yourself!

A Proper Workout

To begin, it is a good idea to start each workout by stretching and/or warming up. This will not only prepare you for your workout session, but will also lessen the chances of suffering an injury. Of course, not all injuries are avoidable, but you should still take preventative measures to keep them to a minimum. If you are suffering from or recovering from an injury, make sure to get the proper amount of rest and learn how to prevent the injury from happening again if possible.

The importance of executing proper form when exercising cannot be emphasized enough. Using correct form, especially while lifting weights, will increase the effectiveness of each exercise and decrease the risk of injury. When possible, perform exercises in front of a mirror so you are able to correct any mistakes you may be unaware of. You may not even realize you are rocking your body during Bicep Curls or not reaching parallel to the floor during your Squats. As you perform each exercise, you should have a mental checklist to avoid bad posture, ensure you are isolating the targeted muscle group(s), and refrain from using improper body mechanics. Slower, controlled movements are safer and more efficient than fast, uncontrolled movements. Proper form should *never* be sacrificed in order to lift heavier weight or squeeze in a few extra reps. Listen to your body, lift properly, and the results will follow.

Working out with a partner can also help guarantee proper form. We do not always see our mistakes; this is precisely why a second pair of eyes can be of use. A quality workout partner will feed you cues such as: not to hold your breath while lifting, do not tuck your chin to your chest, and do not flare your elbows while performing various exercises. If neither you nor your friend is an experienced lifter or athlete, it may be best to seek professional help or research proper form online.

The primary component and, in my opinion, the most important part of any workout routine, is resistance training. Resistance training utilizes free weights, bodyweight exercises, pulley systems, and apparatuses such as resistance bands and medicine balls in order to strengthen and tone muscles. Resistance training is crucial for building lean muscle mass and decreasing body fat. With resistance training, your body is constantly repairing muscle, which in turn, burns calories even while your body is at rest. Whether you are looking to strengthen, tone, improve functionality, lose weight, look more proportionate, or improve your posture, resistance training should be at the forefront of your workout program.

In addition, flexibility is key. Flexibility is not only important while exercising, but for mobility in general. For many years, I ignored stretching and was never even able to touch my toes. And, playing sports and lifting weights caused my body to become even tighter and less pliable over time. Not until I started practicing Yoga did I see improvements in my flexibility, which, in turn, improved my strength and balance. Because flexibility also plays a part in preventing injuries, it should be a top priority for anyone regardless of age or fitness level.

Aerobic exercise is important for keeping your heart strong and functioning properly. The two biggest mistakes gym-goers make when doing cardio is constantly using the same type of machine every time and failing to change up the difficulty during their workout. The body is an incredible machine and is quick to adapt. Interval training, constantly changing the intensity of the exercise, is key while doing cardio. Breaking your workout into intervals will not only challenge you and keep your workout interesting; it will keep your heart rate up more efficiently and increase your blood circulation, thereby strengthening your cardiovascular system.

For athletes with more advanced goals or skills, speed and power are essential. Both of these attributes can be improved through reactive training, also known as plyometrics. In addition to plyometrics, Speed/Agility/Quickness (SAQ) drills may be used to boost your overall athleticism. Box jumps, jump squats, and speed cone drills are just a few examples of this type of training. Although these exercises many not be for everyone, they are a great addition for those looking to become bigger, faster, and stronger!

Finally, similar to how you stretched and warmed up before exercising, it is equally important to stretch and "cool-down" upon finishing your workout. A cool-down period is important for post-workout stretching, recovery, and allowing your heart rate to gradually return to normal. You will feel much better if you take a few minutes after exercising to collect yourself before moving on with your day.

A Few More Pieces to the Puzzle

If you find it helpful, plan your workouts in a notebook or on your phone before getting started each day so you have a clear direction. Utilizing a journal will help prevent you from skipping any desired exercises and is also a great way to monitor your progress and remind yourself of what weights you use for each exercise. As always, preparation is key, and a workout log can save you a lot of time and frustration during your workouts.

Rest days should also be incorporated into your workout program. Rest days are one or more days in a week that an individual *chooses* to not engage in any physical activity so that the body may recover. This is particularly important if your primary form of exercise includes lifting weights. The amount of rest your body requires depends on factors such as your age, fitness level, activities performed, and personal preference. Personally, I only take one day a week off from all physical activity, but that is because I am still in my 20's, healthy, and able to maintain this level of performance without injury or overexertion. Find what works for you and modify your rest schedule accordingly for injuries and illness when necessary.

Whether you choose to take rest days or not, make sure to give your body the proper care it requires to keep performing at the level you desire. Taking time off from the gym can help you avoid "overtraining", which can lead to injuries or hitting a plateau. A plateau is every athlete's worst nightmare besides an injury. A plateau is reached when the body has become accustomed to the level of exertion it is experiencing regularly and is unable to make a breakthrough in strength or some other skill. Getting more rest, changing your diet, and switching up your workouts are some ways to help overcome a plateau.

Variety in your workout plan is key. Switching up your activities and workouts will help you avoid boredom, overtraining, as well as plateaus. Do not be afraid to try new sports or games. Take advantage of the scenery around you whether that means hiking up mountains, going for a run through the city, or completing a grueling workout on the beach. Start each workout with a positive mindset and a plan. Life is all about preparation. When you are prepared, you greatly increase your likelihood of success in anything you are trying to accomplish. Enjoy exercising, improve your quality of life, and never stop moving!

Finally, the mental aspect of exercising is just as important as the physical. If you approach a workout with a negative mindset, you are already setting yourself up for failure. Keep in mind that you are exercising to keep yourself healthy and happy. Whether you like to run, swim, or lift weights, exercise is one of the best forms of stress relief. As opposed to harmful coping methods such as drugs and alcohol, working out is a positive outlet for frustration, anxiety, and anger. Approach each workout with a positive mindset and perform to the best of your ability each time!

I Am ZyckFit: Rachel's Story

Twenty years ago, I signed with a modeling agency straight out of high school. I was naturally tall and lean, but my contract stipulated that I drop another five pounds from my already rail-thin body before I was allowed to work. The shaming I experienced that first day, as my agent lifted and tugged at my clothes, pinching my skin hunting for any fat she could find, fundamentally changed my relationship with my body. It became, in my mind, something flawed and untrustworthy. The thinner I got and the more hunger growled against my ribs and dazed my thinking, the more acceptable my body became to those around me. I wanted to please everyone but I couldn't keep it up. The standards of the fashion industry proved impossible for me to maintain as I aged into my twenties, no matter how aggressively or mercilessly I restricted my calorie intake.

I moved on, grew up and gained weight, found love and had children, but all the while, like many women in our society, I kept weight loss as the ultimate self-improvement goal. I never stopped attempting to get down to that model-approved weight. I kept thinking sometime, eventually, I would have the strength and discipline to get and stay there. I never questioned that agent's judgment of my weight or her right to even have an opinion on it. I thought the less room I took up, the more worthy and beautiful I would become.

When I was first introduced to ZyckFit, weight loss was my primary goal. As months of training went by, though, I ditched the scale as my arbiter of success. I was becoming demonstrably stronger. I completed my first 5K race and felt healthier and was more active than I'd been in a long time. I began looking forward to my sessions at the gym and gained confidence in my ability to complete them. As I gained muscle tone and improved my conditioning, I began to appreciate how unhealthy and short-sighted my former fixation on weight had been. Instead of counting calories, ZyckFit encouraged me to count achievements at the gym and in my day-to-day life as I actively worked to better myself.

ZyckFit, for me, is about transforming my emotional and physical relationship with my body. It is about developing muscles I've never had and loving the sense of growing presence they give me. It is about gaining peace with my limitations and accepting my body, as it exists today. With ZyckFit, I am pursuing athletic and fitness goals instead of scale-driven ones. I am learning to take up space unapologetically and to view my body as an ally, not an enemy.

With ZyckFit, I am striving to make myself better, not thinner, every day.

Chapter 9: Overcoming Obstacles

"It's part of life to have obstacles. It's about overcoming obstacles; that's the key to happiness."

- Herbie Hancock

Although it may sound cliché, I believe God challenges each and every one of us with at least one monumental battle we must conquer at some point in our life if we are to indeed find true peace and happiness. For some, it's an addiction, for others, it's battling a disease, for me it is a constant struggle with food. As discussed in Chapter 7, ever since I can remember, I have had overwhelming anxiety linked to trying new foods. This anxiety causes me to feel repulsed at even the thought of putting a piece of unfamiliar food in my mouth. As a child, adolescent, and even as an adult, I have experienced feelings of nervousness, sweating, and chest tightness when in these situations. Growing up, this problem caused me to skip a number of social events so I could avoid embarrassment and shame. I have been forced to lie countless times to hide my secret because I was never sure how others, even close friends, would perceive me after learning about my problem.

I always knew it was up to me, and me alone, to solve this problem. Even during the short time when I was seeing a therapist, I knew it was an internal conflict that only I could resolve. But how do you overcome something that has been a part of you for years? How do you get over an affliction that has affected you mentally, physically, socially, and emotionally every day for as long as you can remember? How do you fix an internal or external problem you feel you have to face alone because you don't believe even the people who say they understand what you're going through can truly help you?

I consider myself a strong-minded individual, yet, even with my determination to better myself and knowing that I was doing my body harm, I could never bring myself to change my ways. This could have been due to an irrational fear, laziness, or a combination of both. As much as I did not understand or like how my problem affected me, I had become used to it and accepted it. For years, I thought I was going to be stuck in my ways my entire life. But, blaming yourself and feeling sorry for yourself is never going to get you anywhere good in life. And, becoming apathetic or stagnant towards improving yourself is dangerous to your well-being and to your future. There is almost always a solution to your problem if you are willing to search for it and work towards it.

Not until after I graduated college, did I finally make a serious attempt at overcoming this personal conflict. Over the past few years, I have had several friends and family members who have been able to help me feel more comfortable and lessen my anxiety while we tried and tackled new foods together. Some attempts have been tougher than others, but if something doesn't challenge you, it doesn't change you. I refused to settle for being unhappy and embarrassed when dining out or eating at a friend's house. I have come a long way from where I began and I will only continue to improve with time. As I mentioned before, I am still not at the level of comfort I would like to be with food just yet, but I promise you I will not let it get the better of me. I pray the same for you and whatever challenges you are faced with in life!

Internal Strength

The human spirit is unlike any other force on earth. We can withstand and overcome anything with the right attitude. And, we are resilient and capable of bouncing back from a range of hardships including: addiction, persecution, and failure. Every successful person in history has possessed the inner strength and determination necessary to build something from nothing or overcome some degree of struggle in order to find happiness and/or financial freedom. It takes a strong spirit and mental fortitude to overcome and survive all of the challenges life throws at us. Practice meditation to reflect on where you have been and where you are going in life, use positive self-talk to encourage yourself during your day-to-day activities, and set personal goals to constantly push you to improve yourself. There may not always be others around to help you through tough times, therefore, it is important that you are strong enough to support and motivate yourself!

Strength In Numbers

Although the human mind and spirit are capable of remarkable feats, throughout life, there will be times when we require help from others. Some people have support systems they can depend on, while other individuals prefer to be independent and only ask for assistance as a last resort. Contrary to what some may believe, there is no reason to be ashamed of asking others for help or guidance. Whether you receive support from a mentor, a therapist, or a loved one, you can gain an entirely new perspective when you seek counsel from an outside source. Every person has a collection of unique ideas and experiences available to share with us if we are just willing to ask them for help. You never know, the solution to your problem may lie within the mind of the person next to you, and there is only one way to find out!

Dig Deep

There are moments in our lives when we are faced with choices that define our character. These moments determine who we are at our very core. Most of the time, these moments are very trying and the outcome will affect us, possibly, for the rest of our lives. Even when we think we have a pretty solid grasp on who we are, these situations cause us to question everything we think we know about ourselves. Civil rights activist and personal hero of mine, Martin Luther King Jr., said, "The ultimate measure of a man is not where he stands in moments of comfort and convenience, but where he stands at times of challenge and controversy." Whether you are standing up for something you believe in or making a life-changing decision, it is important to follow what your heart tells you is right.

Sometimes in life, you may feel like your back is against the wall and the world is closing in on you. When all seems lost, you may feel doubtful, hopeless, panic-stricken, or afraid. The odds may seem so stacked against you that, at times, you can hardly breathe, and resisting seems futile. In times like these, you have two choices: you can either give up or you can fight for your life! Digging deep requires reaching down to your very core and pulling out every resource at your disposal to come out of a conflict on top. Digging deep requires a "never say die" attitude and doing whatever is necessary to reach that light at the end of the tunnel. Life is what you make of it, and you can either succumb to its challenges, or you can stand up to them and use them as opportunities to improve yourself.

Leaving Your Comfort Zone

Often, we know there are great opportunities available to us if we are just willing to make a change or to sacrifice one or more things in our daily life that we are accustomed to. This may include getting a second job or cutting back on spending money in order to afford a new place to live or to go back to school. Usually, though, it is easier to continue living the same comfortable lifestyle we have been used to for years instead of taking a risk that could benefit us in the long run.

The same applies to fitness, as it is easier to sleep in or go home and relax after work each day instead of going to the gym regularly. It is easier to order take-out or eat at a restaurant than it is to meal prep and cook healthy meals. Putting off a healthy lifestyle may seem passable for a time, but eventually, it will catch up to you. Whether you need to lose weight, stop drinking alcohol, quit smoking, or eat healthier, your future self will thank you for the changes you make today.

With relationships and networking, it can be intimidating to spark conversations with new people, but the return can be priceless. Whether you are working up the nerve to ask the cute girl at the gym out for a date or asking your boss for a raise, you will never know the answer if you don't take initiative! The world is a big place full of people possessing a range of knowledge available to you if you are willing to acquire it through friendships, social media, and networking.

When it comes down to it, leaving your comfort zone is all about overcoming fear: fear of failure and fear of the unknown. There is nothing wrong with being afraid, as long as you do not allow it to control your life. The more accustomed you become to leaving your comfort zone, the more you will enjoy in life and gain experience from the world!

Learn From Failure

From the time we are children, we are taught that it is bad to fail and make mistakes. We are raised to believe that nothing good can come from losing or being wrong. On the contrary, the crushing blow of defeat, although hard to bear at times, makes us stronger. No successful person reached where they are today without failing a number of times. A life without failure leaves an individual weak and inexperienced. It's the challenges and struggles in life that ultimately drive us to be better.

Failures and mistakes are only negative if you allow them to be. If you learn a lesson or take something positive from a setback, then you can make the necessary adjustments to overcome the obstacle or adversity. If you do poorly on a test or don't make it onto a sports team, figure out what you need to improve upon and then capitalize on it the next time you get the chance. You decide whether you accept defeat or rise above whatever challenge it is you are facing in life. There have been a number of times in my life where I got mad or felt sorry for myself when I made a mistake or failed at something. But then that "failure" pushed me to achieve something even greater than my original goal. Nothing good comes from giving up, and in my opinion, giving up is the only true way to fail in life.

Looking to the future, plan on facing many more challenges throughout your lifetime. Understand that *you* are in control of how you react when faced with these conflicts and it is up to *you* to use them as learning experiences. Whether it be failures or successes, or baby steps rather than giant leaps, it is important that you keep moving forward in life. This is the only way to guarantee finding peace and happiness for you and your loved ones. I believe in you and I hope you believe in yourself. Your future is as bright as you allow it to be. Make it a point to go to sleep each night knowing you accomplished something that helped to improve your life. Always remember: Be Better Today Than You Were Yesterday!

Conclusion

Wherever life takes you, regardless of your age, race, gender, or class, never stop improving yourself. Always look for opportunities to learn and to help others. Make the most out of every single day and live a life free of regret. Tell your loved ones you love them as often as you can because tomorrow is not promised. Do what makes you happy and try your hardest to leave a positive legacy once you're gone.

I hope this book helps to change the way you approach life on a daily basis. As always, remember to stay humble, spread positivity, and help others find their way at every opportunity you get. I created ZyckFit because I was tired of all the negativity in the world and I told myself this journey would all be worth it even if I only changed one life. ZyckFit has opened more doors and introduced me to more amazing people than I could have ever imagined. Chasing this dream has been more fulfilling than anything I have ever done in my life and I hope all of you will go after whatever it is that you are passionate about. God bless.

"Live your beliefs and you can turn the world around."
                                          - Henry David Thoreau

Client Testimonials

"I have trained with Tommy Rozycki and ZyckFit for a little under two years now. I started working with Tommy in March 2015 slightly overweight, very depressed, with a chip on my shoulder, and with a little bit of knowledge. We began a training program for a fitness competition at Jupiter Fitness. I started out at a 14.5 BMI. A 42-year-old Type 1 Diabetic woman with depression and emotional challenges. Working with Tommy Rozycki, I was given the motivation and encouragement to adjust my diet and workouts during a 5 month period bringing my BMI to 12.5 and a loss of 8 lbs., all while building lean muscle mass. Tommy is adamant about posture and alignment for safety and structure to reduce risk of injury and to produce symmetrical musculature. I am so very grateful for the opportunity to work with such a knowledgeable and competent fitness trainer. Thank you Tommy Rozycki."- Stevi Q.

"Tommy Rozycki was my very first personal trainer and initially, I was quite nervous about sharing with another person, my failures in the fitness world. These thoughts of nervousness were quickly quieted from the first day Tommy started training me. Tommy was non-judgmental and honest in his approach to set fitness goals for me. It became apparent after several sessions that Tommy is a guy that does his homework for each individual client and accommodates his workouts for that individual's strengths and weaknesses. For many, fitness can be an uphill battle and there is a need for that additional outside inspiration that only comes from those dedicated to enriching others' lives.

Since meeting Tommy, he has been nothing but dedicated to improving my personal goals, level of fitness, and overall well-being. I have only known Tommy a short time, but his motivation in life and in the pursuit of making the world a better place is a true inspiration. ZyckFit is coming up fast in the fitness world and I am excited to see what Tommy Rozycki has to offer the world in the near future." -Tom B.

"Before I started training with Tommy Rozycki, going to the gym was intimidating and felt like defeat. Being a former college athlete and coming back from an injury, I wanted to get back to my former self and I needed someone to support me and push me towards that goal. Tommy was exactly what I needed. His infectious optimism on living a better life and incredible workouts made me enjoy the gym again. Can't wait for more people to experience ZyckFit!"- Cara D.

"In just six short weeks of training with Tommy, I've lost six inches and five pounds of fat. I feel so supported and motivated by him. I look forward to each and every training session because I know I will be both challenged and encouraged by Tommy. His positive attitude is contagious and he has been my biggest cheerleader as I strive to lose the rest of my baby weight. The success I have enjoyed is due to his extensive fitness knowledge and expertise. I am so pleased with the dramatic changes I've seen so far and I know this is just the beginning. I would recommend Tommy to anyone looking to get in shape and have fun while doing it!"- Maria K.

"Jupiter Fitness has one of the best trainers ever: Tommy Rozycki. I love my trainer. He's kind, gentle, and aware of your needs. He listens and works with you. Thank you Tommy for guiding me through. You make me want to be healthy."- Peggy B.

"Tommy Rozycki is such an inspiration to me in helping with my body transformation. I work with Tommy three times a week and have been now for the past three months. I am seeing a wonderful change in my body toning and losing inches all over. If it were not for Tommy and his great push to see results that he strives for with every session that he has put together working for my change, making working out fun and enjoyable even through the pain, I would not be the changing person I am today. I look forward to working with Tommy and I would definitely tell anyone looking to spend the time to improve yourself and self-esteem to make that change in yourself, to do it with the help of Tommy Rozycki. He works to make you a better you..."- Cyndi C.

"Tommy Rozycki has always been an inspirational person in my life, long before ZyckFit! I read his blogs religiously & have recently started personal training with Tommy. The workouts are challenging and I always leave with a sense of accomplishment. What makes everything even more satisfying is Tommy's passion to see myself and others reach their personal goals when it comes to fitness. ZyckFit has not only inspired me to change my body physically, but to maintain a healthier lifestyle in general. I've finally found the motivation I've been looking for & I thank Tommy and ZyckFit for that!"-Amanda F.

"Tommy is a terrific trainer, always enthusiastic and supportive! His methods are straightforward and I always feel like I get a great workout! I would highly recommend him to anyone. He makes staying healthy fun!"- Connie M.

Made in the USA
Columbia, SC
06 July 2022

62742358R00072